CHANGES OF ADDRESS

Born in Cornwall, son of an Estonian wartime refugee, **Philip Gross** has lived in Plymouth, Bristol and South Wales, where he was Professor of Creative Writing at Glamorgan University (USW). He has published twenty-six collections of poetry, eleven with Bloodaxe, including *Between the Islands* (2020), *A Bright Acoustic* (2017); *Love Songs of Carbon* (2015), winner of the Roland Mathias Poetry Award and a Poetry Book Society Recommendation; *Deep Field* (2011), a Poetry Book Society Recommendation; *The Water Table* (2009), winner of the T.S. Eliot Prize; and *Changes of Address: Poems 1980-1998* (2001), his selection from earlier books including *The Ice Factory, Cat's Whisker, The Son of the Duke of Nowhere, I.D.* and *The Wasting Game.* Since *The Air Mines of Mistila* (with Sylvia Kantaris, Bloodaxe Books, 1988), he has been a keen collaborator, most recently with artist Valerie Coffin Price on *A Fold in the River* (2015) and with poet Lesley Saunders on *A Part of the Main* (2018). *I Spy Pinhole Eye* (2009), with photographer Simon Denison, won the Wales Book of the Year Award 2010. He won a Cholmondeley Award in 2017.

His poetry for children includes *Manifold Manor, The All-Nite Café* (winner of the Signal Award 1994), *Scratch City* and *Off Road To Everywhere* (winner of the CLPE Award 2011) and the poetry-science collection *Dark Sky Park* (2018).

PHILIP GROSS

✦

CHANGES
OF ADDRESS
POEMS 1980-1998

BLOODAXE BOOKS

ISBN: 978 1 85224 572 6

First published 2001 by
Bloodaxe Books Ltd,
Eastburn,
South Park,
Hexham,
Northumberland NE46 1BS.

www.bloodaxebooks.com
For further information about Bloodaxe titles
please visit our website and join our mailing list
or write to the above address for a catalogue.

Supported using public funding by
ARTS COUNCIL
ENGLAND

Digital reprint of the 2001 Bloodaxe Books edition.

CONTENTS

ACKNOWLEDGEMENTS

This selection includes poems from the following collections: *Familiars* (Peterloo Poets, 1983), *The Ice Factory* (Faber, 1984), *Cat's Whisker* (Faber, 1987), *The Air Mines of Mistila* (with Sylvia Kantaris, Bloodaxe Books, 1988), *The Son of the Duke of Nowhere* (Faber, 1991), *I.D.* (Faber, 1994), and *The Wasting Game* (Bloodaxe Books, 1998). Some previously uncollected poems have been added to the sections corresponding to those collections.

A Cast of Stones (Digging Deeper Press, 1996) was a collaboration with artists John Eaves and F.J. Kennedy; some of these and other poems in section 5 were written for performance with the group Vanilla Allsorts. *Nature Studies* was published in a limited edition by Yellow Fox Press in 1995 with illustrations by Ros Cuthbert. *A Game of Consequences* was a chain-verse-letter initiated by Philip Gross in 1986, involving 25 other poets, and published in full in *Envoi*.

Other poems not previously published in book form appeared in *The Gregory Awards Anthology 1981 & 1982* (Carcanet, 1982), *Irish Studies Review*, *London Magazine*, *The Orange Dove of Fiji* (Hutchinson, 1989), *Outposts*, *PN Review*, *Poetry Book Society Bulletin*, *Poetry Review*, *Poetry Society Newsletter*, *The Poet's Voice*, *Thumbscrew* and *The Times Literary Supplement*.

New Words for Home was published in the Estonian émigré journal *Tulimuld* in 1983, in Estonian translation by J.K.Gross.

1

THE ICE FACTORY

(1980-84)

New Words for Home

(for Alma Gross 1891-1969, and J.K.Gross, born 1919)

Grey waters, no horizons. Shifting screens
before and after: fog. Belowdecks, machinery
goes on, a guttural ache, and the between-
time lasts, lasts,
                suddenly delivers me
to wharves, warehouses shading out of grey
like rumours in a foreign language, headlines
on a broadsheet washed out in the rain.

§

'Name?' At a trestle desk
I'm dealt a form. Such spaces
to be filled. A pen,
lifted, waits. *'Name?'*
Heavy on my tongue here,
it's a precious coin, our broken
currency.
           'That's all.
Next?' In the yard
I clutch my patiently-
spelled papers. Here
is who I am.

§

Unquiet at my window, dawn. An exodus
of clouds on sheer grey plains.
This country's thin snow, sparse,
ashen, ticks at the pane.
I try to imagine you, waking: streets
of numb drifts, silence, snow-light
without shadows, the chocked ruts
of grey trucks smothered in the night

which you won't mention, seeing clear
enough: the future comes like this.
A year on, your first letter, and I peer
beneath the words for clues. 'We miss
you. Life goes on.' What clerk in uniform

before me sifted through the gentle dross
for guilt? The words pass...and confirm
my fears, the distances, the loss.

§

Strangers, for your family album...She
    conspires a smile; this bright
complete new world is her creation. He

is still her 'foreign gentleman', guest
    to this warm sufficiency,
his stiff tact faltering to tenderness

unnerved by their three-day child.
    Here, now, nothing less,
it demands him, such uncompromised

need. The new life. Five years on they're no
    less strangers. Mother,
would you know your own son now?

§

Your grandchild, grown tall
in a temperate land: how easily
he speaks of rights
and wrongs. Such innocence:
a knock on the door at midnight?
Friends, late, from a party. How I envy him,
and fear for him, who can't imagine why
I jerk awake and scold, from fright.

§

No more, now.
One letter missed, one more not answered,
and before I knew
        you had begun
your silence, taking all that was gone
to yourself. So, then, this was the new
world where I'd be... – what were the words?
'at home'...'in no time'. Only now.

Stations

Each country was a station, more or less the same
– clamour in darkness, brilliant shrieks of steam
ballooning into gloomy arches. Everyone was strange,
the fat man huffed and comical, bleating as if in a dream
'My bags. Where am I?' Sometimes uniforms would change.
Prague...Vienna...Paris...Europe was a game

they should be winning, surely? Town by town, hotels
grew smaller, hosts smiled less, fewer bells rang.
The plumbing was louder, windows smaller to the sky,
back alleys closer, with sunk yards like dried-up wells
where servants clattered, quarrelled and, mysteriously, sang.
His parents grew difficult, not explaining why

when letters came, she cried, and later cried again
when the letters stopped. He stood at a kiosk jostling
among dissonant voices, jowled sour-smelling men,
for a paper Father glanced at, then threw down (rain
speckling the page, the dark stain slowly blossoming,
blotting faces, ranks of print...) More often then

there were voices raised outside his room, or had he dreamed
that? Father and Mother. Le patron and father. Please,
please...And there was Mother, bending close, her hand
steadying him, or herself: 'Listen. You must understand.
Now we have nothing...' And at once, it seemed,
another station: they were struggling trunks (could these

be 'nothing'?) into battlemented piles. Now to play.
'Look at me. I'm king...' He faltered as he saw
hundreds encamped around him, like the tribes of Israel.
Nobody turned. Then a shadow and a roar
of power reined in, steel shrilling on the rail.
The crowd broke round and over him, swept him away.

Snail Paces

As I pry beneath crumbling bricks they come
to light, pale embryos unfolding. Slim
   wands question space,

touch-tentative. They lift small frills
to glide and teeter, balancing their shells
   like the family china. Or brace

on the hawser of themselves; the load stirs
and follows like a shadow. Each shoulders
   his small world like a sack

and strains towards his half-an-inch horizon.
We are less to them than clouds across the sun.
   Beneath the thrush's block

we find them threshed out, littering the grass,
mute violated husks. Bend closer. Pass
   down empty corridors,

intimate windings, moulded by the sheer
day-in-day-out of flesh. Mother of pearled,
   the inner chamber of the ear.

Crab

Shifty, side-skittling, he's on the run,
   the Scissor Man,
with his antique weapons, his stage-wrestler's pose.

And cornered...Cocked, grappling his load
   of menace. Eyes
at the battle slit, glistening. And afraid,

yes, rigid, in his frightful uniform, my tuppenny
   ha'penny samurai...

He squats. Shimmies the quicksand. Melts away.

In Another Part of the Wood...
(Aldermaston)

a world ends, where a swathe of moonlight
silvers a ten-foot wire. The shadow-
cratered heath beyond is bright
as frost. A few slim birches tiptoe
in among cowled pipes, squat tumuli
with concrete cladding, grilles that hum.
It's here, the future's archaeology.
Not a living soul stirs
                         but kids who come
for the fabulous blackberries, powder blue
eggs in deserted nests, huge lunar mushrooms
or on the spongy moss tumps, two by two,
conduct their own experiments.
                                    Hush
hush: two wobbly spooks of steam
twine upwards from their buried vents
and fade apart, like lovers in a dream.

Night-Offering

It was an afterwards, a cindered waste.
Dim skylines crumbling into dusk.
Torn webs of girders. Soft
as snow, in the dead calm, drifts
of ash, a flat sour aftertaste.

Do you hear me? Half in your own dream
you stir beside me. Listen. There
were the survivors, shrink round a thin flame,
hands cradling the glow. What more
to say? I crept near. One of them,

you, turned towards me, lifting from the fire
this fragment that comes with me as I wake:
a twig of blackthorn, bare,
barbed, angular. The palest foam
of blossom breaks along its ragged wire.

The October People

At last, hunger and weariness wore out our fear.
We crept from the forest, found a track and so
came to the village called October. Blown seeds of war,
we were wretched, ragged. Still, they turned to hear
as if expecting us. Their dialect moved close and slow
around us. Yes, there were soldiers, weeks before,

see there, the flag they left... It guttered brown
in the wet wind. Took what they could, promised a new
world, said the farm wife, bringing to the shed
thin broth in an iron bowl. We huddled down
in rough hay sweetness. 'In the morning, you
must go.' 'And you?' 'We bake black bread,

stack wood, salt beef, bury our savings deep...'
The oil wick sputtered. 'After, we repair
the damage? Bitter? As well blame
the leaves for falling.' Falling into sleep
I dreamed of leaves, of smoky pyres that flare
against the dark, brighter as the wind beats on the flame.

Facing the Sea

Low tide and winter. Windows full of Vacancies
outface the empty shingle. Miles of esplanade
whose windy shelters bear scars, elegies

to last year's lusts, lost causes, relegated teams.
The hard boys slouch outside the boarded-up arcade
like ghosts of Bank Holidays past, uneasy dreams.

Nothing awaits them, except time. The air
they breathe is bitter, their radios a thin
irritable whine. They neither speak nor stir

as two intruders inch across the afternoon,
old man and boy. Their stare prickling his skin,
the boy stiffens. Oh, to be someone else, and soon.

To outgrow this half life. To be free
of kindnesses, comforts, tacky threads that bind
him to an out of season childhood. 'History...?'

the old man rambles. His eyes crease but never blink,
as if scanning the sea, as if he were not blind.
'Too grand a gent to visit here. Or so we think.

At your age I'd crossed three frontiers, left behind
all but what wouldn't leave me – a long memory
and a Litvak name. Two burdens, no? You're kind,

despite yourself. You want, and fear, to be alone.
But it goes so quickly, though you won't agree...'
The waves' dull rant goes on, stones grind on stone,

march, countermarch. Beyond the noise
a small far voice still asks: *Papa, they hate
us. Why?* Lost in the roaring. But the boy's

grip tightens, pulls. 'Easy. They smell your fear.
Don't look behind. Look at the sea.' The others wait,
hands idle, toying with a laugh, a stone, a jeer.

Vapourer

A drop of sugar-water, a jam jar on a string
and hush... His flashlight pried among the trees,
jiggled and feinted, then was still. The evening

thickened with scents and chilled, ruffling our hair
as we shrank to one shadow, watched the jam jar swing
spotlit, a moon-faced grin... Conjured from air

they rose: ghost-waltzers, wisps, dissolving in
and out of light, to flirt, a shimmer, there
and gone. Then one was down, grounded and jittering,

ours. Dazzled by sweetness, the frail feathery
scanners fenced. The tinny flitter of a wing
gold-dusted the glass. We muffled its small frenzy,

ran all the way home. In daylight it weighed nothing,
was a husk, a burnt-out fuselage. He staked it tidily
with pins; I thumbed my *Smaller British Moths*, mouthing

a kind of litany: Buff Tip, Pale Tussock, Vapourer...
'Again, tonight?' No, no. I couldn't name it, something
gone between us, our breath frosting the night air.

Allies

A sweet smother of gorse,
pods crackling like flame.
Grasshoppers ratcheting. The thrum
of honey bees recalled the roars
(but distantly) of Flying Fortresses
that cracked the concrete runways
like thin ice. We found no trace

of the airmen, lords of Lucky Strike,
mobbed by the likes of us for gum,
except a washed-out YANKS GO HOME.
They went, with razor blades and Coke
and half the village girls
in tow. The parish in a pique
bulldozed all that was destructible.

Still, their pillboxes squat
in the brambles, low-browed grins
KEEP OUTed and bricked in,
steel hatches rusted shut
(though from beneath the sill
that greenish seep of mud
smelt faintly bestial).

But in a swampy bomb-hole one
slewed backwards, angled
to the sky, door buckled
agape. We hunkered down,
crept crabwise in. And clutched
at the air. Our bearings gone,
we saw each other pitched

at a drunk slant to the floor
and walls, their cocksure verticals
quite unperturbed...We scrabbled
out, blinking. Then roared
our bicycles away towards the faint
heat-shimmer where the runway's parallels
dissolved, the vanishing point.

The Displaced Persons Camp

Lean vigilant faces, sleepless eyes
look up. They sit like children grown
unnaturally, cramped into desks in rows,
and submit to the language of strangers, a stern
new ordering of tenses: is, was,

will be. 'Repeat now, after me.' Each voice
lifts towards clarity, and breaks: waves
on a north shore, a dull bafflement of loss.
'The subtler points – *should*, *might have been* –
will come in time.' The class dismissed,

they are free to sit, or pace the bare
perimeter. Willowherb flares from the dust.
It is neither peace nor war. Beyond the wire
in wide fields, two boys and a dog
race after their own cries. And stop. And stare.

The Victory Dance

The Village Hall in glad rags. The St Juliot
Swing Combo: 'Take your partners, please...'
Three girls to each man. 'And let's not forget
our foreign guests...'
                    The refugees,
shipped from the Camp, clumped round the stove
or drank themselves to tears. But he...

That slight stiff bow. He clicked his heels.
'Permit me the pleasure.' (Imagine, mother. Me.)
He danced like an officer. Yet when the band
came fumbling to a halt, I dared a glance
and caught him lost for words, yes, shy.

Not like that tea time. The great aunts
closed ranks on the settee, the Three Monkeys:
Pru's puddle glasses; Dot's hand cupped
to her bad ear; Vi's nice inquisition, carefully
enunciated as if to a child. The tea unsupped.
He was...correct: 'Madam, I comprehend.
But cannot, as you say, go home.'

Then Jack was demobbed, full of beer
and battles, thumping: 'I don't give a damn
what kind of foreigner....'
                                    I was afraid.
By night, voices pitched from the Quarrymen's
Arms, hard laughter.
                              How could we have stayed?

And yet...A white walled hut. The Chaplain's
gruff brusque blessing. A Best Man
who spoke no English. I thought of you,
and a church awash with hymns and flowers.
('You must learn,' he said, 'you too,
about leavings behind.') That night,
the only guests in the hotel, we ate
in silence, cutlery chinking on our plates,
the landlady vigilant. Then we flung out
past curtained terraces onto the Prom,
past street lamps smoking with blown spray.
I huddled close, thinking, 'Soon it must
be easier. We'll know what to say.'

I lie awake. Rain chafes the window.
Mother, he sleeps huddled, deep,
but has such dreams. What can I do?
He speaks a foreign language in his sleep.

A Honeymoon

The sea was tame but he was clumsy, half afraid.
'Like this,' I laughed and dived, slipped through
to a world without walls, my secret smoky-blue
basement. The mirrored ceiling swaying overhead

shattered, but silently. Pale waterbaby, eyes
and hair wild, topsy-turvy, groping in a dumb-
show of dismay, he fell to me. The dream
broke as his hand gripped mine; we rose

into sun glare, beach cries. He was gentle then
a while, our prints fading off concrete, leading in
to the bare cool hotel room.
                                            Some evenings still
as I wait for his key in the lock I think of thin
blue curtains rippling shut, the sudden chill,
the taste of salt, blue shadows mottling our skin.

A Plague of Jellyfish

One morning the sea blossomed with them, pale *fleurs du mal*
    the Gulf Stream shunted into our too-perfect bay.
        They curdled in the waves
    and blotched the sand. We mourned the spoiled day
by bickering, then sulked, gazed from the harbour wall...

Slow-flouncing, rippling, with movements hardly more
    than a tremor of light they massed, small fantasies
        in see-through lace
    tricked out with poison hair, the sea's
vague figments, flotsam hushed towards the shore,

threats, promises...You reached out, drew us tight
    together as that sightless unrelenting stare
        surrounded us, mauve-veined
    irises flexing as if brought to bear
on unfamiliar distances, our shifts of dark and light.

The Gift

Clogged under cinders, nettles, waste,
it could have been a meteorite
or an old potato. But the mud crust cracked
and flaked away, and look,

it's a perfect ovoid, pearl-
iridescent, seamless,
an immaculate earth-shell.
I raise it to you like cut glass.

And there's an ocean in it. Feel the stir
and fall, the tides taut, quivering,
alive. The air
around us has a salt spray-sting

while deep, safe as a sunken galleon
a dim speck quickens,
hunches, shuffling its cells
like an old man playing patience.

A scroll we cannot read yet, it unfurls
itself, a dark map-labyrinth
filling with dawn. Spark trails
open to thoroughfares, transparent

cities like sleeping hives grow gold-
opaque and audible. Dogs bark,
the traffic starts up like an iron waterfall
and people rise, as we do. Take

this, love, this curious weight
on us. It wants to live.
It seeks us out, says Give
me. And we give, we give.

First Encounter

Abstract and intimate, circling in a void,
you closed on us. The bubble of our world
warped, quivered. You were not to be denied.
A flicker of static, of Morse: yes, yes.
A blip on a dark screen, homing. I can't tell
who called, who answered: you or us.
Or gravity, a dumb inevitable fall,
your lit speck skating over emptiness,

irrupting here, in a dazzling antiseptic cell
with dark before and after. 'It's a girl,'
this lean survivor, streaked with blood and foam.
Now we must wash you into human form,
that venerable head, webbed vellum, purple-
muddied map of a fabulous country, pulsing.

Post Natal

Adrift, and dazed with sleeplessness.
      That cry,
needle-thin, frail, pitiless,
    reels me in. Fed, he
        sleeps; I
push back the curtains on a world of time
    grown strange to me.
A milky slick of smoke hangs low
above empty gardens; only sky
    moves, glacially slow.
        He stirs.
    In our warm lit room,
our honeyed cell, I am calm and numb
as if consoled in mourning, but for whom?
        Friends come
tender and hesitant, eyes bright, bearing flowers.

First Day Out.

Through the hospital gate
the world. The three of us, we're strangers here.
It's all too sudden, an astonishment
of detail, every leaf too clear,

the raddling of old brick
too intricately tooled in smog and sulphur. Tears of rust
commemorate old railings plucked for war.
The pansies' puggy faces thrust

up at the sun. Wires
sew the street together, tingling with news. Two doors
ajar, Mrs 63 and old man 65 conspire
as we pass. They barely pause.

We're not that special
with our new life tender as a wound. She lies unblinking,
an Eskimo doll, dropped here without a word
of the language. Sparrows chinking

like empty bottles, a bus
that grits its gears, a snatch of glottal-sloppy chat, a shout
of airbrakes, sunlight, you and I are all
becoming her: another lifer, out

on parole. Becoming one of us.

A Report of the Burglary

Nothing of value was taken.
But the spirits of the place, the bird-voiced ones,
took fright. They slipped out through the smashed
back window where the night came in.

He came home to find drawers torn out,
clothes scattered. There was nowhere
where the strangers had not been, nothing untouched
or likely to feel clean again. And the silence...

Gone, the gentle presences, who welcomed him
each evening, with an imperceptible
dove-murmuring, who soothed him with a dance
like dust on air, who made the fragments one.

The silence. Every door concealed an emptiness.
He saw peeled paper, splinters, spider-cracks,
some lodging rooms, some bric-à-brac.
The strangeness entered him.

There were investigations. A report was made:
Nothing of value was taken. Now,
when the last of the strangers had gone, he knew
nothing of value remained.

Beside the Reservoir

A surface still as marble. Drystone masonry
runs straight in, under. There is no other shore
but a thin brilliance of mist. One tree
stoops, waist deep. At the small thud of a door

the gulls flush upwards briefly. By the car
two figures stand as if breath-taken. Once
they would have talked, talked, troubling to share
the luminous distance. Now, he points

to bird flecks drifting far out: a precarious
species, winter visitors. She takes his arm,
keeps company, through certain silences
accepted like the need for water, for the drowned farm.

The Curator's Tale

Where do they come from, or go, these few
a rainy afternoon blows in to share
the stillness of stuffed animals? (The kingfisher's
crackling spark, earthed here, is simply blue;
the salmon gapes, embedded stupidly in air.)

Case after case reflects them loitering among
wombat, echidna, axolotl, pygmy shrew;
the Galapagos tortoise, turned to stone
after a lifetime practising; the buttock-faced dugong
that sailors rank with grog and solitude

took for a mermaid. 'That's the stuff'
(my little joke) 'that dreams are made on.'
No one smirks. Ah well. These shrugged-off
species are my stock in trade. Yet if
he (facing the Irish Elk) would turn

and speak, and she (by the dusty clutter
of Fox Cubs At Play) would startle, and respond,
I'd throw the cases open, goldfinches
flirt up in a charm, the grizzled otter
splash clean through the perspex of its pond.

Man and Wife
(Jesse and Susannah Raddall)

Great-grandfather, stiff as a parson you
command my presence. Stern proprieties
buttress you, you them. A family, a farm,
a church, a constitution, all
the hard won hills around you stand

because you do, upright. You must wonder who
this stranger is: what kind of man
never sat at a long oak table, saying grace
over hushed heads, carving knife in hand
with the beef blood on it;

what kind of man never learned through the skin
the leather testament, the print of things
beyond question: belt strap, Ten Commandments;
what kind of man, embarrassed to set his
the last name in your family Bible.

Sons after sons, grown small
before you, felt your great hand raised
like the rainclouds over Cornwall,
tablets of the Law. Old man,
the shadows that you cast

close round you now. Your hands
hang empty. Memories of the soil
you loved and mastered leak
through your fingers. Reach
to me, stranger.
                And I touch

an old photograph. Your black on white
steps back into hundred year twilight.
Speak. 'Alone...I worked my own
salvation, with these hands.' And she?
That pale girl at your side?
                        'Alone.'

                *

Brought to a hard house young,
to a strong cold man who prayed
like thunder, hammering dull

souls to pliant leather. Chill
stony water and a smouldering grate,
the scrubbed slate threshold, the family name,

a bed in a crooked room. The man
stamped his features from you: nine
children. With the last you died

   : a shadow into shadows,
a new voice in the choir of silences.
   Your name, that was his
and your father's, spoken in the empty house,
   sinks without ripple.
What inheritance is yours? Outside,
   the vixen's cry
shivers and stills, once only, far away.

28

The Musical Cottage

An endless Sunday. In the attic room
the solitary child sits. The tune
deliberates each note, each stepping stone
across depths of silence. From the trim

toy chalet two unchanging faces stare,
a mother and father in separate windows,
weather people. He sees more than he knows
as he hinges the roof back on the whirr

and tick of cogs, precise machineries
circling on themselves, clinched and
slowing. As 'Edelweiss' grows hesitant
he shuts his eyes, wonders 'Where is

the music?' Elsewhere. He can catch
only the after-trace, the bright splash
dissolving into ripples where the fish
has gone: beyond him, or too close to touch.

The final note hangs frozen at the lip
of silence.
            Thirty years.
                        It will not drop.

Nursery Rhymes

Mother, you didn't tell me

that the Witch lived on the bomb site down the road, where the House That
Jack Built foundered, rubble-dust and weed; her familiars were the prehistoric
earthmovers with their insect jaws, and cranes like skeletons of knights in
armour swinging slow murderous iron balls...

that the Three Bears grumbled and roared at each other in the house next door;
their Goldilocks, frail changeling daughter, played in the yard, a hundred miles
away; she never spoke to me...

that the Man In The Moon was my Uncle Tom; he stared at his reflection in an
endless sea like the face of a drowned twin; 'Out, get out!' he raged at Wynken,
Blynken, Nod and me; we disturbed his immaculate loneliness...

that Grandmother ate the Wolf; No Hawkers No Pedlars said the gate and she
meant it, with an axe-glint in her eye; one night, small howls and struggles,
then a hush behind her bedroom door; next morning, 'Grandma's gone away';
the Wolf was free...

No, Mother, you didn't tell me the half of it.
Maybe you had forgotten. But I knew.
I always knew.

A Ringside Seat

After the tightrope walker's steely equipoise,
strongmen, cowed famous beasts, a last fanfare,
they jumbled in. Dwarfed by their own noise
they stomped and squabbled through the smoky glare,

loud as a playground. The midget's inconsolable boohoo.
The boss clown's cackle and bark. I shrank
back, touched cool canvas and slipped through
into darkness...

                          And that bright world sank
behind, a big ship passing. Suddenly adrift
I stumbled in mud. Nearby, a guttural hum.
A dog dragged at its chain. A baby coughed
and keened. Dark trailers. Washing on a string.
Stale diesel sweat. And I crouched shivering
by a huge wheel hub; tried to remember home.

The Stadium

A phosphorus white glare
behind the housetops. Out of yards
and ginnels, shadows flowed
together, past my window. Flare

of a match in cupped hands,
embers bobbing. Dark designs.
SPEEDWAY TONIGHT: I heard
the tetchy whoops and whines

of starved machines I never saw.
Next day the track was scribbled,
rucked; the grass here dulled
with dust, there parched to straw;

the corrugated shed (GRANDSTAND
1s 6d) patched with a sign
for Whiffs, a platform on a soon-
to-be-disused branch line.

Chip papers, fag ends, emptiness
with a sweet scorched smell.
And silence? No, a subtle
niggling in my ear, a tinnitus:

grasshoppers, coming out like stars
till the whole field thrilled
with brittle simmering applause
– abruptly stilled.

'Oy!' Cinders crunched:
an oily giant with a jerrycan.
'Lost summat, boy?'
he grinned. I up and ran.

Powder Mills

(Dartmoor, 1873)

Built for explosions –
a roof light as a crust of lichen,
    walls like bastions.

Made to shed
their hobnails at the door, the men
    entered 'shod

like parsons'. Brimstone
in the air, and the fine black dust
    a narrow sun-

slant might reveal
ascending round their heads, a bright host.
    Rumbling of the wheels.

Yet Silas who would down
his day's victuals at one sitting 'lest
    I perish before noon'

never missed a day
'for it minds me of God's mercy. And besides
    the work is dry.'

A thump in the air,
less heard than felt. They pause. Outside
    the pot-bellied mortar

fumes. An overseer
gauges the proving-shot's trajectory. Two score
    yards: the powder

is approved. A rabbit's
white scut jiggles through the gorse, and fear
    keeps within limits,

knows its place.
It is another century. Larks shrill and rise,
    rise to the emptiness of space.

The Ice Factory

Not a great deal is known about this minor industry,
which appears to have had a short life.
HELEN HARRIS,
Industrial Archaeology of Dartmoor.

A hush like a shut Bible. Father: 'Grace
will wait...' The latch clacks. Our stare
lifts from our cold meat, from the empty place
to the door...and Cousin Joseph. His chair
grates on the flags, and Father: 'Now
let us pray...'
            Who knew him? Slow
to speak or laugh, slow at the plough,
some kind of fool, they said. I'd go
to fetch him in from the topmost field:
'This place don't give us nothing free
but rain. So Father says.'
            He smiled.
November, bitter drizzle. He
went up the hillside as the cloud came down.
December, snow penned us behind doors.
The first clear morning, we'd see thin
tracks, wavering slightly, up into the moor.
In March, I followed. Jumbled stone
in a windy hollow; black peat-water riffling;
a turf-wadded hut. 'You've come alone?'
He prised the door, 'Then look.' Nothing,
I saw nothing, or a glistening black, before
the ice-cold took my breath. His chill
smile: 'Things aren't always where
they're needed. Are we, girl?'
            April,
he was gone. Was seen halfway to town,
cart lumbering under bales of moss and straw,
steaming and dripping. 'Taking water down,'
they laughed. 'Thought that's what river's for.'
Then nothing. Though the horse was found
by the docks where the tall ships come. All year
they traded stories – 'mad', 'enlisted', 'drowned'
– and tell them still for any stranger's beer
since the farm's gone back to moor.

And now
this flimsy envelope: *New York*. Inside,
'My father would have wished...'
He was rich, somehow.
Had grandsons. Mentioned me before he died.

2
CAT'S WHISKER

(1985-87)

Hearing Voices

Stones don't *have*, they *are*, voices: the clear
chapel bass of a granite house above the sea,
the burr of sandstone, or a slate-flagged floor
tuning itself to bootsteps...while I'm sitting here
buttonholed by bricks and mortar, their eighty
year old gossip I can't catch or quite ignore:

What did the doctor say? What happened in the end?
I thought: I'll strip one room to quietness.
It peeled in whispers. Melancholic brown, a fuss
of paisley, nursery pink, like tones of voice a friend
or widower would spot in a crowd, years later: Yes,
that's her; it wasn't *what* she said...Deciduous

mulched tatters, clogging underfoot. Me, me!
my blade grates plaster. It calls up the taste
of dereliction, bashed-out walls with skin-
deep patchwork open to the sky, our curiosity,
the wrecking ball. My smug new paper waits.
Sweep up the dead. Then how shall I begin?

Cat's Whisker

   'Cat got your tongue?'
Go on, I thought, laugh! (They did.) *She
understands.* Charmer and snake in one,
she padded in and coiled beside me.

   I could talk to her
with her lithe knowing silences,
no questions asked, only the whurr
of a finely tuned apparatus

   idling. 'Is it true?'
I whispered. 'You see ghosts?' She seemed
to smile. (Then again, cats always do.)
But the family's day-long 'atmospheres'

pained her: that slow build
and itch of static in grown-up altitudes
above my head. She flexed. Yawned. Bristled.
We were bad music to her. Yes, she knew

what wavelengths lace the air.
But how? The first twitch of her whiskers
was the sign. She'd be stroked anywhere
but there. *Cat's whisker*: the encyclopaedia

showed a crystal set, a family
bent close. Cack-rackle-hiss: a jumbling
rush of atmospherics...Then, haltingly
at first, this small voice, coming through.

Revelations

It should have been the glassy sea
where seraphim cast down their crowns
or something. It was stone. I was thirteen.
Something had to change, so why not now,

my first Communion? As the gloomy swell
of the organ washed me to the altar rail
I glimpsed her, kneeling: how her sensible
shoe gaped back a little from her heel

which was white and thin. I tried to equate
the polystyrene wafer gummed to the roof
of my mouth with any earthly taste,
with any bread or body that I knew.

I stared at the polished marble till my eyes
mazed, and it was the surface of a pond,
tensed. Slow mud-swirls began to rise
like clouds about to part, beneath, beyond.

Loving Spoonful

Over the top they go, the do-or-die brigade.
They fall in their thousands, feebly threshing.
The fittest go bludgeoning on. They spread
like spilt milk from a moment's indiscretion.

They're a smear on the microscope slide.
Wipe it clean. So much for....was it lust?
A righteous going forth to multiply?
What sort of God whips in this Exodus,

what grizzle-thighed games master hacking *Go
for it, lads!* from the touchline?
                                        No,
it's us, the love we make. Or think we do.
It makes us, using me, love, using you.

Post Marks
(Estonia, 1985)

1 *A Snow Scene*

The stamp brags: Salyut girdling the earth
with flags and red tape. *Two weeks in the air?*
the postmark whispers, *On whose desk?* Beneath,
the address argues from general to particular:
state, city, street (as cameras might zoom in
on hundred-yard irregularities from space)
to a number and a name. Inside, a snow scene
and a Christmas greeting: 'PEACE.

Good news. Our Vovka is come home.
Is better. We walk a little out today
in Progress Park. Each twig bears snow,
its own load. (See, the camera tells no lie!)
All earth is held still, even the stream.
There are bright bubbles in the ice.
He stands, I stand, till we are numb,
not to disturb. We hope for peace.'

Can that be all? This game of patience
is her life. *Better? Home?* No cipher
at the censor's desk could trust words less.
Camera? Lie? She means more
than she says. I slam the papers
on my desk. *Peace? Numb?* We'll shake
it out of her...
                    'What is there left to hide?'
she shrugs. 'What do you want me to say?
Is better, is better. Can it be denied?'

2 *From the Other Side*

'It's a quiet life.
I play myself at chess
turning the board each move
imagining a deathless
master opposite, say
Alekhine...though Alekhine
nearly did for me
in '44 (after your time).
Some Youth League cub
doing his good deeds mistook
my Alekhine's Der Kampf
for quite another book.
I was frogmarched off.
By luck the Commissar
was a player, of sorts.
He kept me all night there
at a trestle table in a room
without windows. Doors
clanged to, feet clicked
and I glimpsed corridors.
I played my best ever:
I let him win. Towards dawn
he shouted , 'You don't *try!*'
A sacrifice, I swore. And won.
He shook my hand: 'We play
again. After the war.'

More often, though,
I try to guess what your
moves might have been.
I never had your flair.

You'd sacrifice the lot;
you'd break through or
be damned. I was the plodder
and glad of a draw,
the quiet life.
                    So here
I sit, the last of us,
on the edge of my world,
staring out across
the State Farm's great
wide-opened squares
of wheat. Or give the dead
another game. Where
in the world are you?
Did you really break through?
And would I post this,
could I, if I knew?'

3 *English as a Foreign Language*

'Dear Sir, You will not know me but I wish you to.
I study English two years. How I wish for some one
I may correspond to. Mother says this might
to be misunderstood. I know in others tongue
are so many things I may not say. But I shall use
a dictionary. Why should not peoples to each other write?

Here see my photograph. The Upper School Work Unit
at the Heroes of October State Farm. Last left at back
besides the many potatoes, he in the spectacle is me.
I am not strong in sport. And some time I am sad
for the brothers and sisters I have not. I am unique.
I keep old things, as stamps. I save small countries

that are not now. (May I cut off your Queen's head
if you write?) Also I have Grandfather's red and white
chess men though I play not, a boar's tusk, a accordion,
a bullet from the Patriotic War, a piece of meteorite
that Father sent me (my best treasure) from Siberia.
He labours in important projects, and is long gone.

Please write, if it is permitted. Tell me of your
own self. And please teach me a good idiom to startle
my teachers. For I confess, my grades are poor.
I could not live in English. You can say too many little
different things. Here it is simpler. Where you have four
or five words, some time we have none at all.'

The Balance
(for Helen Gamsa)

    It narrows down to us
or so it seems. Grafting your tree
to mine the genealogist makes history
    converge to a precarious   .
    balance: man and wife,
yours/mine, left/right. Even that patch
gone threadbare on each side: we match
    the frayed ends, life
    for life, Gentile for Jew.
What separated Abraham, packed west
from Riga on a slow train (all the rest
    implied: *d*. 1942)
    from Karl (*d*. 1943)
whose line went east to peter out somewhere
beyond Irkutsk? A few miles, then a war.
    'My enemy's enemy...'
    can't quite make them friends
though the difference between one cattle truck
and another is as history, hindsight or luck
    dictates. So much depends.
    The only point of balancing
is us. 'He who preserves one soul,' teased old
Maimonides, 'is as one who preserves the world.'
    If each equates with everything
    how do we count? I'm afraid,
my love, if there's a balance it won't be
the kind we keep, but that in which we
    hang, and shall be weighed.

41

Baltic Amber

It's a drop from a tall well of light
in a forest of vertical shadows, a resinous
   stillness. It's warm to the touch
in my palm, at your throat; hospitable to us

   as to the ant, older than Christendom,
preserved in its sweet pine sap. Where are
   the hordes of Tartary, the Knights
of the Teutonic Order, Wallenstein, the Tsar?

   Wear it close, night and day, a charm
against history. It takes nothing to heart:
   flipped up on the tideless shingle,
scavenged for a hoard, for booty; bartered,

   a gewgaw to the broad and brilliant
piazzas of the south. Then clutched in flight
   by a dark-haired child, in crowds,
on platforms, cobbles, quays. Crossing by night

   see her sleep; the ship creaks
swaying like a forest and her fingers, thin
   as a grandmother's, clutch the stone
like life. Tonight it lies against your skin.

A Breton Dance

A stone grey town with a name like a bell:
Tinteniac. Was this the place? The time?
The square was empty, blinkered for the night.
On, out, beyond a hoarding ZONE INDUSTRIELLE

we drove between vacant Euro-factories,
beached white whales. And this was it:
a lorry park like a floodlit airstrip,
and the dancers. Then the bark and wheeze

of the *bombarde* cut the hubbub, keen
as bad cider. The shock of it flowed
among them, losing young and old
in a pattern of spirals, yet a single line.

A hundred heel-and-toes became one long
slow shudder, like a snake down all its scales.
We backed away. It flexed its coils.
The pipe throbbed round and round and on

into the night, needling, defying rhyme,
reason, development or cure: the sweet ache
of dreaming yourself a nation. When you wake
the place is always wrong. That, or the time.

Hole in the Ground
(Delabole)

New times, new voices, pebbledash on slate
– what's it to me? I'm passing through
not like those strangers on the trim estate
that was Lobb's field. Yes, but I know
that snicket at the lane's end, and I let
it lead me, back, to what the cottages
conceal. I duck the Danger sign to edge

close, closer…Whack, and jackdaws sheer
off scolding across half a mile of emptiness.
I almost catch the ricketing of winding gear,
the shudder and whump of a blast. Almost.
They dug a small mountain out of here
and camped in the slag: sullen, swart,
'close as one slate to t'other', short

of shank and temper; drunk, 'a pestilence'
to good farm folk, until a lonely Methodist
unfurled damnation. A mutinous silence.
Then one voice, a slow joke, 'Mister,
we ben in the Pit a long time since.'
A dropped stone, rousing to a grim
accord of echoes, a Revival hymn.

*

'We expect them, fervently: the saints,
those stern tremendous men
with eyes like boreholes, waterfalls of beard,
a steady hand
to split souls cleanly at one blow.
They will descend
any day, in thunderclouds of steam
from the Great Western Railway, crying: Where
the pulpit? Where the text? And we
shall lead them to the quarry's edge.
Behold, the earth laid open at the page,
at the difficult passage. They will make it clear.'

                    *

    In the slate museum
he's on show, preserved, the last.
    He turns from me
to question the grain, his chisel tip
    nosing the spot,
the mallet almost gentle in his fist.
    He knocks. The slab
comes open crisply with a sigh.
    He leans ajar
two perfect tablets as if I
    might read. Stooked
sheaves behind him, they recede
    to headstones packed
aslant in chapel plots; low slate-
    scaled terraces
which darken under rain, roofs
    shivering to steel.
He stares back. Neither of us moves.

Stonepecker

At the crack
of dawn a shadow slopes
up the lane to the quarry:
old Jope.

Rack-rack.
What's that kickstarts
like the whack and trip
of a dicky heart?

A snuff of smoke,
a burnt stone smell.
Rackatack bashes on
like a pecker in Hell.

Gone broke.
No copper no zinc no coal.
Got the richest vein of nothing
in a county full of holes.

Behind his back
it's: Old Man Jope got no hope.
Scrubs his face with a stone for soap.
Tied the knot with a length of rope...

No joke.
He had a missus who nobody saw.
He let her out once
in 1954.

She ran amuck
in Plymouth, ran off with a sailor.
He's been digging ever since.
Going to catch them in Australia.

Come unstuck.
The vicar came enquiring for his soul.
Damned if he could find it.
Must have lost it down the hole.

Got the quack
up from Bodmin to examine his head.
It was granite to the core
with a little trace of lead.

There's the shack
where he sits in tumbledown weather.
Stone dust and diesel grease
hold it together.

Take a peek.
Hush. The rackatack stops.
You can hear claws click
when a jackdaw hops.

Lob a brick
down the lifelong drop.
Quick
run run away and don't look back

'cos the stonepecker's after you
CRACK.

Moore

(Recumbent Figure, 1934)

unnh   grunnh?   grohh
wassamatter? wh'am I? who the? No
go'way. I was dreaming. I was deep.
Where was I? Dancing. Arm in arm in...she.
All round me. We was waltzing, slow
slow, round and round. And suddenly
there's all this...unstuff. Is it sky?
I never asked. You did this to me
damn you. You made me this: I

am. But I can take it. Mass-
culine I ham, a bullwork. Charlie Atlas
torse, the strangth of clunched hands,
nubbled biceps (feel that!) in a man-
to-manly buddy-hug.
                        But mateless,
muzzlebound, manhandling
unthings. Unnnh. A not-
hole in the heart. You, you abandoned
me, you left me wanting...what?

The words gro wrong. It's a terribore
think, this onliness, this wanting....more.
There must be others, no? No eyes to see,
I not-quite-touch them, close. Quick flimsy
curious things, warm breaths...

                                        I'm floored,
yes down but no not out – a lourdly
drunk who might yet lurge upright, embrace
the emptiness and astonish the dance-floor
with a coup of (how to put it?) grace.

Apple Gatherers
(Stanley Spencer, 1913)

   Each night, for the men,
a dole of stoat's-piss cider in the barn.
   Women had homes to go to.

   Dossing in straw
his head was filled with apples, apples. He saw
   Martha, plain dull Martha,

   in a smudged green sunlight
coming steady as a queen to her confinement,
   apron bellied full

   of fruit. Then Boy Jack
goosed her, hooting as her hands went up
   and all the apples spilled

   out from her, sound-
lessly, endlessly, helplessly down.
   They'd bruise and spoil.

   At dawn the slow ache
of the job resumed. Tree by tree, back to back
   they worked closer, within reach.

   Neither turned or spoke
as he slipped her the prize of his pick.
   Their forearms touched.

   What passed between them?
In a freak of sunlight they saw generations
   like as apples, spilling

from them, heat-
tranced puppets, bobbing, aching in a sweet
    druggy smell of fermentation.

    She saw a frump of a girl
who coveted one beauty for herself
    and bit. She saw the slug

    in its flesh-pit, glutting
in all innocence. He saw the rootling
    snout of the old pink sow,

    shrill piglets squabbling
into her as she rolled – her flabby grin,
    her battery of dugs – and

    Master's coming, quick!
he saw a boy thrash the pigs off with a stick.
    The apple dropped and lay.

    The picture's dated
1913. Next year she'd be picking again
    alongside raw boys and old men.

Little Dancer
(after Degas)

She's stopped in her tracks, her face
up, eyes and lips
                        tight, braced
for what? Applause? A slap, more like.
Or a kiss from a dusty uncle. Not in spite
but because of the ash-brittled lace
that frills her hips
                        she's irreversibly
exposed,
            betwixt and between,
                                    not quite
a child, her body not quite dragooned into grace,
her stocking puckered at one knee...

48

She's very old,
                fourteen,
                          and cast in bronze.
Her plinth is wired. After we've gone
and the attendant snicks the lights out one
by one, a black box on the wall
considers her. It watches, all
night, as her mother might have done.

Tar Boilers

Sleepwalkers
wading in bright mist
or deep sea divers
shuffling silt, they cuss
the dodgy burner.
First sun prinks the frost.
    Each word becomes visible.

They crank
the handle and the dribbly
cauldron gulps, volcanic.
Gloss-black slurry
nudges down the shute
steaming like fresh manure,
    serviceable.

Now they tamp
a square plot. The roller
bumbles and clanks
and seams it matt.
The driver huffs and stamps.
A thermos steams in his mitt.
    Cars cough awake.

A small boy waits,
the pavement quaking at his feet.
He buffs a bright
new minted ha'penny:
1958.
Now? Now. He tweaks it in.
    Signed, sealed. He runs away.

Here Today

I've lost them, scrabbling in the leaves,
small and clear, already further gone
than I'd realised, down an avenue of trees
as down a rabbit hole or telescope. One

stalks a squirrel with a tail like smoke
in its I'm-a-little-teapot pose; away
it switchbacks, stop-go, quick-quick-slow.
Kid brother has come up against

immensity, his gaze corkscrewed up
the leathery torsions of a chestnut bole,
up helplessly. One more twist and plop,
he'll be flat on his back...No,

that was me, or so the story went,
fond family apocrypha. It sends me
leafing back through the concordances.
Here's a touch of the bark, its peppery

tang. But there's no trace
of me, touching; still less of whoever
watched, as I watch now. No face
to the gaze. What gets preserved is trivia

like that camera obscura, some Victorian
inventor's toy. We paid our pence to lean
above a pale disc pitted like the moon
and clacked the shutter open; green

resolved to trees and there, a couple
dodged from cover, larking silently,
then caught each other, then looked up
and pointed...straight at me.

Slap, and a ripe burr ricochets
to burst at my feet. It shocks
me to my senses. Here today
and...let's leave it at that. 'Look,

look!' Their hands are full to running over:
chestnuts, glossy-dark as good antiques.
We'll crack them, roast them on a fire
and they'll be sweet.

A Cornish Saint

They can't be serious, those two-a-penny saints
    washed up like holy jetsam – no mere boats
for them but millstones, coffins, kegs. So delicate
    Saint Ia had to float
in on a leaf. Their visitations stopped abruptly

as the trippers' now. St Ives is emptied like a till
    and counted. Stiff winds scrub the town.
Summer timetables tatter and flap; awnings rattle
    up, are battened down
as the season stows itself away, no time for me

and precious little shelter. Ia's chapel on the cliff
    is padlocked and the path slips ledge
to ledge, nowhere to go but down, brittle thrift
    for handholds. At the edge
deep water thumps and swashes, almost within reach.

There's a wicked glitter underfoot. I'm not the first.
    Someone lugged bottles here and sat
and drank, and watched, and drank, with a thirst
    he couldn't fathom; then smashed
every last one. Green glass lapped him like the sea

and then? Was that *her* on the water as the tide-
    race tightened to the point, as the Godrevy
light began to pry. 'Oh pray for us, unauthorised
    ridiculous Saint Ia, in these heavy
times...' And did she beckon: Come with me...?

Magic Lantern

(Bishop Rock, Scilly)

Flash... Dusk. Shadows scud off the sea;
the boulders shrill. To westward, the reef
malingers, sucking its teeth thoughtfully.

Flash... Men on the rock. Brought on the tide
by sceptical boatmen they pick, hack, drive piles
till waves slop their knees. Or crouch inside

their low stone barrack. Gales thud spray
on the thatch. One morning they creep out to see
a year's hard labour swatted clean away.

Flash... Calm, now. A bright regatta
noses through the flounce of ten-foot weed.
Boatmen unload their top-hat-frock-coat betters,

bustles teeter and a small string orchestra
assembles its parts, unsteadily. A thin waltz
ebbs and flows as, first, the Lord Proprietor

and his Lady, then each in rank, gravely,
circumspectly, dance. Against the waves' one-two
their rhythm counters: one-two-three one-two-three.

Flash... Polite applause. They wait for light to fade.
Ashore, the navvies drink up six months' pay
and swear Never Again. Out here, a toast – *To Trade*

And Navigation – as the lighthouse lifts the shadows
with its first flash, then, in its own cockeyed time,
quick-quick-slow, and wait, and wait, *quick-slow*.

Flash... Wrecks decrease; a local industry
goes down. The islands empty. Still, the boulders
shrill: storm petrels ghost in off the sea.

The Lookout
(for J.K.G.)

It's a rain-swabbed cell, niched high
   in a shale slab headland
   on a wrecking coast. Inside,
dark like the dark inside the eye.

It's a post not manned this century.
   Three arched windows
   west, south, east
take in the brilliant deceptions of the sea

in sunlight, or how it mulls the glow
   now as the snaggled shore
   beds down in shadow.
Waves muster, sharpening the narrow

spit of black where one last fisherman
   shoulders his tackle to push
   up the steep scree path
to here. His breath drags. He stoops in

shucking his bag. He tastes the cool
   church smell of slate.
   Where he stood
pale foamings pucker and spill

till there's nothing. And suddenly
   he's chilled. It's late.
   He should be going but
can't move. The long *hush* of the sea

has silenced him. A wink of light
   traces the coast road.
   Now it swivels, fans
up, up and seaward, as if taking flight.

Shadow on the Water
(for Bob Devereux)

We surprised each other.
Leaving friends asleep,
the house sunk in breathing,
I slipped out. And there
he stood, knee deep
in grey reflection: brother
heron, rumpled stiltman
with a stoop. One look
askance; he shrugged,
neck cricked, wings hauling,
gone. But not before
I knew him, *mon*
semblable, gangle-
bodied stalker, shadow
on the water, dumb professor
of the quick eye and the slow
step. He lost his kill.
I broke the mirror.

From the Fast Train

The town falls by the wayside. Gone astray
in the urban outback, our racketing dulls
to an auctioneer's gabble. Rails splay
into rusty sidings. Long grass rankles.
There's a rash of fireweed, smatterings of may

and there, gone feral on clinker, a shock
of lupins, wild colonials. Was that a goat
cropping the scrub beside a landlocked
quarter acre? Scratched earth and a rain butt?
Thin smoke tippling from a corrugated shack

no path leads to or from? And who'd
be waiting there, who'd be at home
nursing a Coronation mug, tea stewed
to a metallic tang? Yes, that's him.
'Such a time,' he'd say. 'What kept you?'

Tabernacle Yard

Strict and particular, dwindling
fiercely, they met '8 p.m.
God Willing' in a firebrick
kennel up a cul-de-sac
so tight to the railway's cinder
scarp they timed a Psalm –

The Lord reigns; let the earth quake;
let the people tremble –
to contend with the 8.15.
Through narrow panes
they glimpsed the fireman's face
bent to his chink of Hell.

'So shall the world be borne away,
smoke streaming after fire,
the Romish temples, the gin palaces,
the music halls, the horseless
carriages. Thunder by night. Yea,
brothers, let us prophesy!'

The end is always nigh; theirs came
and went. The padlock on the gate
fat as a fobwatch clinks and swings.
A rusty block and tackle hangs
in chains. Wrecks sans wings, lights, chrome,
everything, our write-offs wait

for GOFF & SON, the resurrection
men who promise BODY WORK (beneath,
NO JOB TOO SMALL) but never seem
to come, except to underfeed
one sidelong mean Alsatian.
It smiles humbly, with its teeth.

The Private Sector

FABRICATIONS, the sign says, up an alley
that could be the scene of a crime.
The workforce has gone cannily
to ground. Whatever their business is
it's none of mine.
Under charked brick arches
on the quarter hour, each shed
fills with a labyrinthine
grumbling as a train crumps overhead.

Face up, spraddled beneath a van
there's a body in a boiler suit.
That monkey wrench might be the weapon.
But it's only oil
puddling beside him, and his foot
taps reggae, his mouth shapes the wail.
Head swollen with a Rasta tam, he's
wired to far-off sounds, deaf-mute
to the joiners' operatic agonies.

A power saw whinges and stutters.
They're feeding the caged blade.
It digs in, slobbering, but is
wrestled free; it runs shrill.
The planks are clattered out and laid
to rest in the sun. The smell, still
warm, turns the mechanic's head.
He smiles. We've got it made.
It's simple as sliced bread.

Man and Wife II
(Mary and Thomas Holmes)

'Stoke up the fire.'
She was not to be gainsaid.
Brushing words aside
her hand stubbed There!
and There! She made
us understand. 'The bureau?'

Yes. 'The drawer?' Yes
yes. We were so slow
bringing to light the yellowed
trove of albums: pressed
flower smiles of distant
aunts; old men who stared
as if they knew. 'You want
to look?' No! And a blunt
jab: On the fire. She spared
nobody, least of all
herself. That night
she died. Raking the grate
we salvaged one stiff curl
of silvery ash. Some quite
unknowable boy soldier's
face was ghosted there,
blacked up, benighted,
hair turned white
as zinc, like hers.

                    *

A son of the Empire, fallen
     among Cornishmen,
          to a narrow one-
street village and a tribe of in-laws
     closed against you.
          Your colonial tan
soon bleached in the slatey rain.
     By the time I knew,
          you had shrunk away
as near invisible as flesh permits,
     the ghost of a military
          bearing. (No defence:
I wouldn't let you be, with my
     'But what *is* India?')
          India was words
like *Bangalore... Madras...* The hiss
     like gas of Nag,
          king cobra.
Rikki-Tikki-Tavi juggling
     Nagaina's egg,
          an unexploded shell.
Your Gurkha kukri. ('Don't you tell
     Grandma I showed
          you this...')

The sip-sigh of a stainless blade
   from its scabbard.
   'Did you fight?'
I stroked its edge. 'Did you kill?'
   Another long word:
   ceremonial...
which led you to Bombay,
   'a brave show',
   a bazaar of hooters,
flags and bands, three cheers
   for a plucky mongoose
   mascot in the colours
as the troopship hauled away
   for France.
            They say
your face was one raw scar
   from mustard gas.

   I never saw.

The Ghost Trap

We climbed for weeks. After the armpit weather of Barrackpur
the air was like iced water: we were gasping, we were
gulping breaths that stung our throats, yet craving more.

Then the tree cover broke, and the clouds: first sight
of the mountains, ranged against us, the whole skyline
rucked, keen as if freshly broken, dangerously bright.

It flashed back our hearsay like a heliograph: the Tsar's
agents in Lhasa...whispers in the Dalai Lama's ear...
moves in the Great Game...remember Kabul? the Afghan wars?

We pushed closer, into the encirclement, crunching on ice-
locked screes that creaked under the weight of sunlight.
And we climbed. Once, in the shadow of a precipice

we saw a bright snow flurry cresting from its lip. The track
was a rumour, all the gullies blind. Then deep in the rocks
a flicker and a drip alerted us. The stream ran on, not back.

We had crossed over. 'Hip hip...' I started. (I was young.)
No cheer came. The stillness was miles high. And a stone-
slip whispered. Echoes snicked round and round and on.

The word nobody breathed (yes, they remembered) was *Kabul* –
the expedition slaughtered, one man dragged home by his mule.
We eyed the overhangs, expecting the shot, the manmade rockfall

    for five days. Chonk.
  We wheeled. In the mist, chonk
chonk. We piled into cover just as something
    like a short-arsed cow
  botched out of greasy string
shambled by, its belled head bobbing. Now
    we saw the huts,
  a village slunk among boulders,
patched about with hides; no windows, no doors
    but a single hole
  where the smoke dribbled out,
where flat urchin faces peeped, then shrilled

and our way was blocked. Squat raggedy
bundles of men – were they men? –
swarmed and chittered. The Captain's voice
stayed them a moment; they faltered, then

flared. They were coming. At their head
a yappy pug-dog of a man, preposterous
with brass and bangles clanking, made
wild passes with an antique blunderbuss

and Fire! the Captain gave the word.
The mob shuddered. They seemed to be
locked in a slow dance, swaying,
as the Maxim gun tracked patiently

back, forth, back. So this is war,
I thought dimly. Why don't they run?
Then their back rank broke. The crush
subsided with a groan. We hurried on.

And Lhasa? The Forbidden City was a slum.
   Sewers slopped the palace walls.
     His Most Serene
Magnificence, we were informed, was not at home.
   The Captain thundered our demands
     to underlings
who nodded and nodded and smiled. Why had we come,
   they asked, so laden and so far? Yes
     they would sign
a paper if it pleased us...And there was nothing
   more to say or stay for.
     As we turned
to go, one spoke in English. 'A question, sirs?
   What manner of being
     is a *Tsar*?'

We scoured the monastery for food.
No meat. Scrapings of meal.
It was a rat run without corridors,
insulting sense as one bare cell
led to another, or a bare courtyard

or...Pungent nothingness. I stumbled,
cursed, then saw. It was a shrine
scabby with jewels. And there he was,
bunched in his robe. I'd never seen
a man so old, so utterly feeble.

He came straight at me. He was daft
with terror, brandishing this thing,
this...what? A rickety fly swat
or a spider web of sticks and string.
I stood, I almost laughed,

I was stern, I shouted, all
but wept. He would not stop.
When I pushed him he was light
as dust. He crumpled up
without a sound against the wall.

. . .

'Ghost Trap (Tibet).' It was in Tunbridge Wells,
some auction room. After fifty years, the very article.
I must have twitched. 'Sold to the Colonel!'

and the auctioneer came blathering like the fool
he is. 'Of course. Old India man like you.
Just up your street.' So here it is. No real value,

common as dirt out there apparently. Do what you will
with it when I'm gone. But now? On the bedside table,
yes, within reach. Damned silly, isn't it? But still...

Coelacanth

Après le déluge, moi...

Survivor of survivors
(was the Rock of Ages cleft for *this*?)

he's found his niche,
his bunker, his last ditch.

Evolution blunders overhead;
the wreckage comes sifting down.

He paces midnight mud plains
on stiff fin-struts, almost legs.

He'll get it right next time.

Meanwhile there's the dark and the cold
and the tons per square inch to hold him

tight. (Dredged up, he'd split
his sides.) On the face of the waters

life flirts, glances, shudders
to and fro, like shoals of wind.

The Clever Children

'The chicken? Or the egg?' Their father
teased them on their way to bed.
They lay awake for hours, those clever
children. Then one little egghead said:

'Inside the shell, the embryonic hen
has got all her cells in her, even the cell
of her egg, within which...' So on, in, on
in time, to the smallest conceivable! Well,

now they couldn't sleep. They had to see
the ultimate egg, the egg of the future. On the way
how many breakages, unwanted omelettes, casually
discarded chickens? At last, there it lay

so tiny, so precious, so shimmeringly slight
it made them feel tremendous, like a pride
of giants. Now to sleep, but...'Wait!'
said one. Yes? 'What's inside?'

So they split it. What hatched out?
'Quick,' they yammered, 'put it back again.'
But those clever children couldn't, not
with all the king's horses, all the king's men.

Son and Heir

He's up. And off, a tipsy
   tightrope turn
juggling with gravity.
   The ascent of man
starts here. Like one spotlit

   he makes his stand
on the brink of a big-top
   drop. The ground
sways. One false step
   and...

Will he take it stonily
   like Sitting Bull?
Like holy Job? Or melancholy
   Charlie, fall-
guy to the old joke? Will he

   heck! He's baby-bald
Khrushchev, blaming a shoe
   on the diplomatic table:
'WE WILL BURY YOU...'

   No joke. He will.

Boys Fishing

   He's got it, all the nonchalance
of a flick knife. Ask his mates. What he wants

   he wants. See how they turn to him.
He's snagged a gout of weed and swings it in

   slap at their feet. They flinch
then scrum to see it twitch: a mud-green three-inch

   crab that bridles free of weed,
huffs, bubbles at the sky and can't conceive

   of such as him who casually, ac-
curately heels his new black boot down crack!

   It's mushed, still bubbling, legs awry,
as he turns back to his rod. Go on, ask him why.

   'Cause I didn't want it. Ten
years old, he is, and unassailable. An innocent.

A Mercy

Do something, she said.
                    The demolition
site had been a bomb blast in slow motion

and still smouldered. A faulty streetlamp
fizzled and pinked and – there! – that blank

rasp, clearly now: a cry about the size
and weight of a baby's. I picked and prised

among tipped slabs and shadows, till I saw
where it lay. I wrapped it gingerly. Indoors,

unswaddled, it curled and quivered. Fleas
snap-crackled in its spines. Leaves,

ash and clay crusted the lumpy bag
of a body that it somehow could not drag

as if I'd never freed it. Something inside
was crushed but not severed. And it cried.

DO something!
                   She watched as I filled
a rusty pail. I nudged it in. It scrabbled,

wallowed, useless. I rammed it under,
holding my own breath and holding, longer

than seemed possible, till with a shudder
it went slack. A silvery-quick globe of air

slipped from its mouth, broke surface
with a pock. I looked up. But her face

was turned away.

The Cloud Chamber
(for Nigel Crooks, 1951-1972)

'You crack an atom, what's left? Particles,
bits. It's like Meccano: proton, neutron, quark.
Don't you see…?'
              The things you knew.
The rest of us set our horizon at the girls'
school down the road. Whatever you
dreamed of, you left us in the dark.
('I couldn't follow him,' one friend confessed
after the fact, then '*Why?* The waste, the waste!'
then again 'Did he *know* something we don't?')

'There's nothing to it.' Your pale face
lit on a smile. 'A molecule? A galaxy?
Nothing but little obstacles in space.'
As clear as mud. Just for a moment, though,
your laughter shook me. It was wild –
a touch of vertigo. I saw the solid world
come unput at our feet. I didn't see

the logic: how you would leave behind
friends, family, a fixed address,
even your books, until
              one tactful line
in the Hatched-Matched-and-Despatched: *Died*

Suddenly. No note, no clue,
you left us nothing, as if we were less
than nothing (little obstacles?) to you.
'Why?' You'd have shrugged; worse, smiled:

'Why anything?' What could I say?
Except…one icy-crisp November night
we watched for meteors, crouched back to back
for warmth. 'There!' 'Where?' 'Too late.'
A scatter-fall of debris from deep space.
I felt you shivering. I saw the track
in the cloud chamber. Bits. The waste.
The toll of microseconds. Particle decay.

Flying Dreams

(Philip Smythe Raddall, 'missing' 1943)

A dinky yellow dump-truck rusts
in brisk spring sun, up to its knees
in rubble and daisies. The straight thrust
   of a tarmac strip runs out
    to grass, an order countermanded
    suddenly or overcome by doubt.
The outfield yawns, in service only
to be empty, stuck in a *drôle de guerre*.
The windsock wags its trunk in memory
   of braver days, whenever they were.
It points. It points to me.

There's a throat-clearing clatter, thinned
by distance, and a rickety single file
of trainers nudges out to sniff the wind,
   snub-nosed. They toe the line
   in cough-and-shuffle unison.
   One shudders and shifts; its whine
bites. And I'm hooked. The hop into flight
is nothing to that lift of pitch, that pulse,
that will to go. Going, gone, he's high
   off the edge of the hilltop; up he pulls
by his bootstraps into blustery bright

emptiness. And I've lost him. Phil,
it's you, boy uncle. It's your after-image
winking on an RAF-blue sky, the thrill
   of it, the pathos. Dreams. I grew
    up in your hand-me-downs, your shadow
    and your name. I ached to follow you.
At the Air Show, I decided to enlist.
I'd fly. But I was only six, and besides,
short-sighted.
               Overhead an engine skips
  a beat; he's dipping back and rides
in as on surf. The undercarriage tips

turf and he flinches, doesn't slow
but bucks and revs again. (Somewhere
an officer's voices is crackling: No.
   Again. Till it's perfect.) Lifts,
   wingtips wobbling. He hops the hedge
   and away. I gasp. You'd have laughed:

'The flying's easy. It's the ground
that gets you in the end...' Yes,
other uncles, never you. No matter how
    they fade and fall to reminiscences
you won't come down, not now.

*

'Phil? One of the Few?
Not him. No, Bomber Command.
Ground crew.
He never thought to fly

only they lost so many.
Tail-end Charlie on a Wellington.
Proud? He was twenty...'
As I take my leave

her look halts me: 'Tonight
as you walked in
I saw him, to the life.
Put you in uniform...'

Outside, I'm shivering: fight
or flight. There's the usual skyline
on the usual rust of light.
And suddenly, the moon.

*

Numb, effing
at the gut
gripe cold, bone
cracking din,
the cramp. No
where to look
but back. Slow
grey silk sea
in moon frost
then a blacked
out coastline
blotting foam
then
        flak! Ripped
glitter chills
and the shock
wave butts you.

Bastards! Hung
in a steep
manoeuvre
you look down
where scattered
seeds bud flame
and bloom. Then
fire! Fumble
with the gun.
Can't. Numb. Ice
bitches it.
(Night fighters
closing.) Ice
patterns craze
the glass. Fire!
But it feels
like ice.
                    Ten
thousand dead
in Hamburg
(Do you read
me? Do you..?)
and among
the missing
here's your name.

                         *

Fire-storm: a brave new word.
Just drub enough bombs in
(we did it, Phil) and fire
feeds on itself, becomes its own
bellows and furnace. It was war,

it was orders, it was work well done.
Sleep, after all those long nights
waiting for the moon. Your ash sifts down
with dockers, mothers, dreaming Hitler brats.
It was Hamburg, it was Dresden,

a new world. We did it, Phil. Sleep
if you can. Will that blaze
smelt names, ranks, all our histories
together, till they lie at peace?
Sleep sound. I'll have the dreams.

Charlot's War

As the front falls back towards Armentieres
the asylum keepers flit. Their charges, touched
or dumb, come out slowly, blinking. Where

is all the world going? What's this slow ruck
on the high road: bikes, prams, barrows stacked
with pots, pans, piglets, children? A khaki truck

blares. In the dust, a Madonna and Child in one,
Mimette rocks herself. Jean waves and grins. Charlot,
six-foot slab-featured farmer's son,

sees the ooze of fear made flesh. He bolts.
He's away across ploughed fields, ducking low
to the earth that smells of...what?

He forgets. Now he pants in a ditch. He slops
his face with scummy water, laps a bellyful
without mug or manners, then studies the plops

of small frogs for an hour, Upright again,
he finds a land that's no man's but his own.
Nearby, a cow helves to a pitch of pain.

He smells milk frothed warm in a jug
and follows. But the farm is shuttered blind,
a trap: there's a whinging snarl. A starved dog

dances on its rope like a baited bear, Run,
Charlot, run. The forest soothes him, but beyond
he drops, bristling. There's a wounded truck. Its man,

a soldier, bends beside it, thoughtfully
slashing each tyre, then beats each headlight in,
then unloads from the cab – Charlot cranes to see –

a wireless with a grinning dial and knobs like eyes –
Charlot gapes to hear – and with a pickaxe handle
crunches, then steps back, not feeling Charlot rise

behind him. Big hands clasp, and wring. Now mile
on mile Charlot stumbles and sobs. And there's
a cottage. He tires abruptly like a child

come home. It's almost welcoming the way the door
gives at one shove, into cool stale dark.
He wakes hours later, on the parlour floor

to thunder, close. He creaks open the shutters.
Light catches an iron cage. He rips it. Three
canaries flop out. Two are dead. One flutters

weakly, crazily. He soothes it, sets it free.

3
GAMES OF CONSEQUENCE

Blank Page, Marginal Notes

ground zero
is the blank page
nothing

half a mile
the zone of simple
irremediable cries

a mile or two
first childish fumblings: 'a kind
of flash', 'a sort of boom'

fifty miles distant, miles
high, the language becomes almost lyrical:
'like a living thing', 'the mouth of Hell, 'but...beautiful'

*

It's a question of technique: the calibration
of charged matter, priming of the fickle
fissile words, tact, timing. At the critical
mass there's nothing but the elegant equation.

Roget gives forty-one synonyms for the verb
Die, seventy-five for Kill...'Don't bother me
with conscientious scruples,' said Enrico Fermi.
'After all, the thing is technically superb.'

*

Oh, Little Boy,
you had no mother,
no midwife, no wetnurse.
Little wonder

you grew mean.
Conceived of in equations
you stepped like Athene
from the big man's

headache, fully armed.
If you grew high and mighty,
little wonder, if you stood
erect precociously

to punch a fist
clean through the under
belly of the sky
it's little wonder

your grandfather
Einstein grieved,
'I should have been
a watchmaker.'

You stamped your foot
above Hiroshima.
Our childhood died.
Oh, little man…

         *

Mushroom? Why not coral? Burning bush?
Crown of thorns? I keep it on my shelf
as I write. Find words for me,
it grins. Forget yourself.
A skull? A cudgel? And I'm dumb,
foolish and for a flash (poor
Yorick) feel what fills that numb-
skull: hunger, hunger. 'More,'
as cities crumpling like sea, 'More,' sea
like white birds scattered, birds
like ash, 'More,' feasts of simile,
a fat world ripe with words
bow down before it: death's head.
It consumes them, and it is not fed.

Early Warning

This is it. No panic, no sirens. A boy shies a stone.
A girl blows her dandelion out in one. Footballers, bright
confetti in an updraught, rise and dangle. Each alone
we squint towards the ball, the seed, the what or why
    that won't (we should have known)
    reach ground. A braid of white
undoes itself across the poster-paint-blue sky,
a finger trailed in water, a ripped seam of foam.
At last...as if grey birds that strangers' hands ignite
from vans in distant lay-bys had come ghosting home.

       At last...That's all:
  a feeling curiously like relief,
like peace on earth, just as the missiles fall.
The moment before moments will be fused
to ever after...and I wake, in time. *Complicity*
before the fact! I think. *What did I do?*

from A Game of Consequences

      Grandmother watched the wind. Between the lines of cirrus
      she read storms at sea. We have a lot to learn.
      The forecast comes on sinister with reassurances:
we may drink the rain. The wind has swung back west and we
are not to worry. There is no cause for concern
except being told so...No, the count is not significantly
      above normal. Soon enough, this *will* seem normal, mark
      their words. These sacks of cumulus, trundled overland
      a hundred miles, still fat with the Atlantic, used to hark
me back to the rinse of waves, to cliffs scrubbed bare
as facts. Now I toy with the map: a small leak fanned
from Hinkley by a mild wind from the west, and where
      would we be? Here, in the zone marked *Uninhabitable*
      For Twenty Years. Another superstitious game to play...
      Don't search the sky for omens. On the parlour wall
three china ducks rise, sinister – from left to right.
But we are not to worry. As Grandmother used to say
catching my face disfigured by rage, fear or spite,
      'One day the wind'll change. You'll stay that way.'

    . . .

It's an all-night hotspot: The Submarine.
I've gatecrashed on a circling of the damned
beneath the polar ice. Yes, it's a dream
    but whose? With telly-goggled eyes
    the lads lounge, able-bodied. It's the boredom
    they've been smoking leaks that greyish haze
in strained air. There's a treble hiss
above a hushed bass drumming. (Don't disturb
the neighbours. It could be the death of us.)
    Above each bunk, taped to the metal wall,
    pink Pets spill tits; an airbrushed bum
    pouts peachy as a ripe split world.
A smoke wisp drifts through a bulkhead door
sketching a girl in a shrink-wrap dress,
bruised eyes, a morning-sickness pallor,
    and fades like the ghost she's already become
    on shore, haunting some married quarters.
    Biceps like bags of wet cement, tattooed MUM,
a cropped boy cracks his knuckles and yawns
so close I can study the zit that bugged him
shaving. Missiles itch in their tubes. One
    of these days, we'll see who's dreaming.

A Few Words for Walt Whitman

Too much, all that booming and brawling. When I tried to speak your lines
I stumbled in them. Jostled in the ranks, I couldn't stop or follow.
I wouldn't consent to the big sweaty bear hug of your voice. All too much,

the sour physical tang of it, smoke, ether, blood, all that 'old mad joy'.
Now I'm writing this, small, in a small black notebook. I'm often afraid.

If I glimpse you at all, it's through the breaches between words
when both sides falter, facing for a moment not each other but...
(You observed this yourself: 'not a gun was fired – all was petrified –

it was more solemn and awful than all the roar and slaughter.')
Here you come, big man, dresser of wounds, clumsy lover of all this,
just when I need you, through the rubble that might turn out to be anywhere,

between canvas stretchers in a tent, between bleeps in the Cardiac Ward
when the monitor stutters, then weeps, where we can't choose but meet,
all the tongues of the world thrown down around us and what's left to say?

What This Hand Did

This is the one. This is the hand
that made a castle in the sand.
   When the tide turned present to past
   this hand tried to hold it fast.
When drops trickled through its grip
this hand let the moment slip.
   When the hour was getting late
   this hand reached out for its mate.
When that touch was no relief
two hands tangled in their grief.
   When grief was too much to bear
   two hands wrung themselves in prayer.
When the prayer had been ignored
one hand fastened on a sword.
   When its knuckles went bone white
   this hand carved up wrong and right.
When the laws began to twist
this hand made an iron fist.
   When the laws began to break
   this hand grabbed what it could take.
When the whole world's banks went bust
this hand scratched the moon for dust.
   When the seasons came undone
   this hand tried to forge the sun.
When that sun began to rise
this hand tried to shield its eyes.

This hand. This one.
What has it done? What has it done?

Threads

Yes, but what about the spiders? There'll be no
    sheds, pelmets, crannies under stairs,
        no room for supercargo
    in the bunkers, whose conditioned air
will certainly exclude flies. Where will they go?

Seven years' bad luck, to kill a spider.... (Yes,
    just one.) How many species of Arachnidae,
        how many money-spinners,
    mummy-swaddlers, house-guests, high-
wire-walkers, air-fishers, scuttlers, secret sharers?

How many threads to pick up? A small brocaded bead
    sewn into her work, she makes the pattern
        new each day, Eve's-
    dropper, baglady, common-or-garden
Dame Diademata. She taps into tingling wires to read

all the news that's fit to eat. She's a radio astronomer
    sifting the hum of space; here's the slight
        bleat of a quasar,
    the crumpling of a sun, a distant Try
Try Try Again...
                    Today, a first stiffening of the air

and the webs touched in white on the privet...Such
    glass bead games, such Honiton lace,
        such moon dust.
    But empty: the pattern was lost
for this year, at least. They would crumble at my touch.

from The Air Mines of Mistila
(to Sylvia Kantaris with thanks for the game)

Marked Route

'What tour could be complete
without a glimpse of them? Mistila's mountain air
has been mined immemorially. The miners, it is known,
can breathe no other. In our thriving cities of the plain
they die. It was to protect this folk our President-
      For-Life set up the Reservation.

      What heart of stone would not stir
to see the lone air-miner in the dawn, setting foot
to the sheer rock wall, not to return for weeks, or ever?
Or to catch, as you depart, the glimmer of their scattered
camp fires or, faint in the wind, their old laments
      that are untranslatable and without end.

      They may approach, or speak.
Take care. Their language sounds like ours
yet has different meanings. They may woo your camera
for small gifts. It is not advisable to leave your car.
This brochure is approved by the Military Council.
      Keep to the marked route. Enjoy your stay.'

      The page twitched into flame,
no warmth. Stone-dark. Chill pricklings of stars.
And absences of stars, that were mountains, trees or...
One spoke: 'You are lost.' 'Help me. Where is my car?'
'They have towed it away already. That is over. Come...'
There was a goat-hair blanket, human smells. 'Where
      are you taking me?' 'Nowhere. You are here.'

      That night their breath warmed me.
The next, I ranted. They brought green bitter tea.
The next, I tried silence. Someone burred a jew's harp
out into the dark. The next, I could not sleep. 'Xencha!'
a grin beneath bushbaby eyes piped: 'Me!' She told me
      stories. I could have been the child.

How a man struck a vein of air so pure
he forgot himself and turned sculptor. With his treasure
in a goatskin bag, he left for the plain. In a roadside bar,
the show: it hung for a moment, an intricate nothing in the fug,
then dissolved from the edges. They stoned him. 'Xencha?
      Is this true?' 'True? Yes! For me...'

How an old man cuts deep, deeper shafts
in higher mountains, which is why he grows weary
in the body, climbing back. How they come on nubs of thunder,
thin strata of human cries, the wingbeats of extinct condors
fossilised in air. ('Yes,' frowns Xencha, 'you are learning
      but not perfect. Say not *they*, but *we*.')

A Passing

Jasta is gone.
Tomorrow we will feed
his body to the air.
We are weaving his cradle.

Tonight there is haste.
He went without a word
watching for his dole
of cactus porridge, the ladle

dripping. He forgot
so many little things
he will be sure to miss
when he arrives. So Xencha

little one must run
being young and supple-
soft to squirm through openings
too small for sense.

We sway her in a circle.
We rock her from arm to arm.
This is the Hive of Ghosts;
we swathe her in a nasal hum

till her big eyes close. 'Now,
little meltwater minnow,
run!' her mother whispers.
'Overtake the old one

on the steep track.
Remind him of our names.
Say we sigh good air for him.
Say his goats go well. And say

here are his tools, the noun
'whetstone', the verb 'to sprag'.
Also 'dirigible' and 'flimflam':
he will want to play.

Give him his treasure.
Then, oh watch for the way
and the footing, hurry back.'
Unsurely, Xencha stands

as if for blind man's buff.
She threads a maze between
no obstacles to where he lies.
She folds into his hands

his nickel-plated key ring
with the ritual words
worn smooth by fingering:
FORD MOTORS.

With it, he used to say,
if he had not mislaid the key,
he would open all our doors.
If we had doors.

Dr Crampfold's Complaint

Dear Sirs, While sensible of the trust your august institution has reposed
      in me
I have to report that my contribution to the World Digest of Critical
      Socio-philology
will be delayed. My expenses here are nil, as are my findings. This – can
      one strictly call
it a *community*? – has nothing one might properly term a *custom*. I have
      explained to them that all
known cultures have such things. They express surprise, or interest (or are
      simply polite)
and say 'You are a great professor of this. Teach us. May we do a custom
      this very night?'
Their dialect appears a hybrid of the common tongue and an uncommon
      desire to confound.
'Our roots are in the air,' they say. 'The leaves reach the earth and brush it
      with a speaking sound.'
The deep structure of their grammar resembles the labyrinth of shafts,
      mostly disused,
that litter these slopes. 'The wind,' they say, 'strays into them and cries
      aloud, confused,
like a hundred whales.' They have never seen a whale. They have forty
    words for a certain bean
they never eat. 'Forty beans make only wind,' they say. 'Please tell us
      what we mean.'

Lishka and the Chief of Police

There she sat, hawking her nothings in my market square
among the goat-butchers, grog-shops, lentil-dumpling-
vendors (crooks to a man but at least they sell *something*
if only a hangover). Why had nobody reported her?

'Why?' I shouted. They shuffled and muttered. She sat,
empty-handed, bare legs in the dust. Of course... No-
where but in this gopher-hole would men stoop so low,
to touch one of them. 'Take her away,' I spat.

'Where, Sir? The jail has fallen down.' I had her shut
in the one safe house. My own. There she would see my gun,
my brass medal (from the old regime), see I was someone
not to be snubbed with that dumb blue stare. 'Slut!'

I cried. 'What do you charge them for your...services?'
She emptied her bag: six beans, a nail, some amber wax,
a penny whistle...'Each pays with what they have.
So will you.' 'Hussy! Don't forget whose house this is!

When my wife comes from the city she will smell the smell.
Go wash. Make yourself decent.' I never meant...But there
she stood, in night-sky black, see pearls for stars –
my mother's mourning dress. I slapped her and she fell

across the bed. 'Bitch!' As I straddled her, curiously
numb, I was high, breathless, near vertigo, hacking away
at something cold but insubstantial. It gave. As I came
I lost my grip. I fell. I would fall for ever. 'Help me...'

stretched from my lips. I clutched about to find her
gone. Only the black dress, stained, torn, rumpled.
And a tapping at the locked door: 'Sir? Is there struggle?
Please, what are my orders? What has become, Chief Sir?'

A Perfect Match

Dear Father Superior, Do not believe
the salivations of the Press. The good souls of Mistila
are attached remarkably, I almost said *religiously*,
to what we must call marriage. They do it again and again.
No, don't misunderstand. Monogamy
is, in their phrase, 'the only serious way to play.'
The bond is neither carnal love, nor rank, nor property
but what Crampfold terms the Principle of Mutual Astonishment
which has to be demonstrated once a year.
Folk converge from miles off for 'a good match'. Nor
are they mere spectators, for they hoot and jeer
at predictable gestures. Infidelity is slow-hand-clapped.

At the least hint of collusion the match
is declared null and void. Some couples play safe:
long silence punctuated by a few non-sequiturs, much
like marriage elsewhere. In the olden days, I am told,
      weddings were truly gladiatorial affairs.
Fatalities were not unknown. One famous bride-to-be
staged the spectacular illusion of a funeral pyre where-
in she hurled herself to inflame her beau's ardour
      with pre-emptive suttee. Duly stupefied,
he leaped into the flames she had spoken out of air;
he tripped on a boulder, cracked his head and died.
'But beautifully,' the old ones shake their heads and sigh.
      The rematch I witnessed was tame
by these standards. He brought a ripple from the crowd
with his juggling with starfish, blindfold. All the same,
her Maori oaths seemed a trifle studied. At the end
      something more seemed called for. I
stepped forward, sprinkling from my little phial
of holy water. The crowd erupted, lifting us head high,
the three of us, and declared us most astonishingly wed.
      I have tried to explain my vows.
They slap their thighs and roll about and cry, 'Too much!
The game is over!' What am I supposed to do? And how?
Father, I stand in mortal need of your advice.'

Alys, Wife of the Chief of Police

My love came from the mountains
He has done me right and wrong
I know not him nor yet my child
My time will not be long

Dusk. The village draws into itself, and apart:
here, a lit window; there, a door opens and shuts;
a child is shushed; dogs yap from yard to yard
and someone is singing. Alys stands. She would be
a shadow if she could, the long black shawl
across her face. If Max passed now, he would see
nobody, another peasant. But hush, that song...

So dark he stood at the courtyard gate
The wind wiped away his song
A drink, he begged, my throat is dry
I shall not hold you long

Maxwell had knelt once. 'Be my First Lady. A Chief
of Police is a somebody. His wife is a somebody else.'
The jeep could run her into town. Do not lose your chic,
he said. And later: do not spend your time with nobodies.
Except on official occasions. Do not be seen without a hat.
Now he was out at pistol practise. She could hear the peevish
peck of his gun up the hillside. And that song...

There's nowhere in the world, he said
Our baby will belong
But I'll return the day he's born
And take my child along

Behind that wall would be a garden, and a slim girl
singing her heart out straight to the sky. The Alys-
shadow peeped. There, by an iron mangle was a terrible
gross woman lading washing. As she slapped a shirt
and trousers off the stone. a brief male outline dried
away. The pistol-swats had stopped. As Alys turned
for home the hag threw back her head; a pure voice sang...

Now the night comes from the mountains
And I know not right nor wrong
Where is my love? Where is my child?
My time will not be long.

The Last Sight of Xencha

'What's a story when there's no one left to listen?'
She tosses the question into a mossy adit
like a stone.'I am,'

says a voice. She peers in. At the fringe of light
sits a man of no colour; hair, beard, skin,
even his eyes are white.

'Uncle! I thought I'd made you up. So you're true!'
Far below, yellow excavators flense the hill.
The wan man nods, 'And you?

All this is finished. Go to the plain. Down there
those eyes of your will serve you well,
whereas here...' She stares

into the dark a long time, then 'Uncle? Can you sing?
Do you dance? No? Then I'll teach you. Wait...'
she bobs back, 'One more thing.'

By a rusty stream, she fills her bowl to the brim.
She leaves her reflection in it.
Then she follows him.

The Dancing

'Once upon a time, there was a savage tribe
who danced for rain. Danced, maybe days, maybe
weeks. Some fell exhausted. In the end, what joy:

the rains! Now, *we* know that it always rains there
every month or two. Always has, always will.

But could it be they just *liked* dancing?'

from The Case of Thomas Prote

Last Entry

Prote. Thomas Prote. The missing man.
We have a date. Approximate location.
The survey ship *Prometheus*. And a journal
in his own trim punctilious hand:

'Left Ascension Island. Some rain.
Wednesday 3rd October, 1879.'
Chaste facts, no gossip, no emotion.
'Work interrupted. Small typhoon.'

We have his findings. As the dredge
brought up its thimblefuls of sludge
for his microscope, he sketched it all,
diatoms mainly, page on page

of crystalline geometries,
a silt of snowflakes, every one
a death. Then, three months out
he lets a new word slip: 'a *lovely*

specimen!' And gradually his hand
betrays a change. Soon he admits
the pronoun I. With so much
emptiness around him, he expands

until: 'Landfall! Such scenes
of Gothick desolation. Near the island
what might seem at first a tide race
parts to our bows and reveals

itself a multitude of creatures,
chasing hither and thither, seemingly
in pure delight. At dusk
the penguins, for such they are,

throng the rocks, where they raise
a weird unceasing wailing. One dives,
hundreds follow, marking the dark sea
with phosphorescent trails.

Tomorrow, at first light, we land...'
Then is only the empty page
they say he stared at afterwards,
for here the entries end.

Among the Snake Worshippers of Brazil
(The Wide World Magazine, September 1899)

The beastly stench! The brazen gleam of sweat!
          In that torment of drums,
more rainstorm than rhythm, dark flesh grew bright.
          Some jabbered in tongues,
in shrill macaw voices. Some wrestled serpents,
          slow as circus strongmen
bending iron bars. One clutched a wriggling
          rooster with no head
like an uncorked wineskin. Then he, the preacher
          in a frock coat tattered
like a fringe of seaweed strode towards me.
          He was stooped and lean
and white! 'Brother,' he cried, wiping steam
          from his thin wire spectacles.
'What shame brings you here? Blood on your hands?
          I say unto you:
all that is living wades in gore and excrement.
          Many fall, few rise.
But see...' A mulatto woman staggered, rigid,
          backwards into many arms,
a snake snug to her throat. 'This one
          is in the Little Death.
She is perfect. Her soul is a tabula rasa,
          washed in the Blood...'
But for the blot of it that clung to his palm
          the way he shook my hand
we might have been meeting on a Sunday afternoon
          at his club in the Strand...

A Coffee House in Murrenstrand, 1929

'Leben? Uberleben! To live over and above. Mere man
merely lives. The Ubermensch *survives!*'
          Gusts from the sea
shovelled rain on the glass. The Professor
broke his words like bread. Nobody stirred
          but his two hench-boys: Rudi
with a flush of acne and the ghost
of Trotsky's beard, the young berserker Bruno,
          Left and Right,
wolfhound and mastiff, each slavering inside
but still leashed to their master. With small
          wire glasses, smaller eyes,
his hair gone pale as if scorched at the roots,
he was never seen to eat, or fed on self-neglect
          like a saint. He paced
and preached: 'Master Darwin might blench
at the great Coming he foreshadows...' 'Yes,
          the Proletariat!' 'The Race!'
The dog boys chimed their discord. 'Children,
children...' he was chuckling through the crash
          of splintered chairs. Next day
on the strand, they were at heel. A paperchase
of gulls came heckling; one by one they dropped
          and strutted in his train.
The Professor stooped to toss them crusts
like pearls of wisdom, with the lordliness
          of pure disdain.

FROM *On Why Books Be An Abomination And An Instrument Of The Devil*
All Excepting The Good Book What Is Not The Work Of Human Hands

How you may ask came a poor unletterd chap as I
on such speckilations. Near seventy years since I went cabin boy
on board I think The Promise Thus. Never did discover
what port we were bound but sailed in circles nowhere
for months and in Godforsaken latitudes but what
I do recall is we had as supercargo a young Mister Pratt.
There was a scholar mad for his books I always said
and was I not shewn right soon enough they turned his head.
On Rookery Island it was we put ashore all stones

it was but in the midst huge grass in tussocks overgrown
prodigious from the droppings of many birds I suppose.
But master Pratt says he must see his self and in he goes.
All day we waits till Captain swears profane Damned Booby
lost his self and picks me being small for the search party.
All a maze it were inside all overhung and every inch
thick with nests and droppings birds and eggs and chicks
all screaming every time you put your foot and the smell
like a fishwifes vomit pardon me and like to souls in Hell
birds slashing at our knees youd not believe those beaks
like cutlasses and in our ears that endless torment shriek.
We backd out quick and took a tot to fortify us then
we built a fire and waited. After dark then very sudden
the grass crashd apart he stumbled out there he stood
all trembling like in a rage and up to the waist in blood
egg stuff and stinking but his eyes like Moses come
down from the mountain. From then he was mad and dumb.

Translated

Egg drool in warm fat
clouding, and the yolk a wrinkled sun;
in it, a smudge-speck, a comma of blood:

the scene of the crime,
while on the radio a spruce voice scrapes this
from the empty barrel of the Falklands war:

how an Argentine landing party
on an unclaimed islet came upon
a young man, curiously whiskered and in tatters

not of uniform but of a frock coat.
He had been dead, it seemed, for no time,
lying at his ease in a makeshift nest of tussock grass

and looking, if a poor
translation can be trusted, 'as if he had fallen
out of one dream straight into another...'

The Painter of the Lake

He slaps a quick grey drench
across the sky. As it weeps
he works his colours in,

old man with misty glasses
and a little box of tricks
that folds out neat bright tinctures.

A crowd begins to gather, shyly:
children, dogs, then half
the village at a little distance.

Our lake, our two mountains.
He gives them back to us
perfect. Every Sunday afternoon.

He makes them as they are.
He washes out his brushes
in the lake, which is why

it keeps its blue-green-grey,
year in, year out.
Only today

he has not come. Instead
your coach arrives scattering
the goats. Your faces gaze

from its green-smoked glass
like carp. Our children
find their own reflections

in your hubcaps. But
the painter? Is he ill?
Oh, if he dies

what will you make of us?

In the Foothills of Synaesthesia

'Zyvrosht,'
they say. The woman hews a slice.
Many shadowy children, aunts and farmhands watch.

He hesitates:
Bread? She frowns, then slips it
to him like a kindness. 'Nja. Zyvrosht!' It has the taste

of the first bread ever.
Now she tips a stone jug, nodding:
'Oshru.' The sounds trickle through his fingers.

He has said too much
and made no sense. They shake their heads
and pat him and leave him alone. He listens to the dust

in the village square,
The clatter of sunlight on the cracked tiles,
the flicker of a boy's voice down the ochre track to where

quick syllables of glitter
spell 'lake' for no one else to hear.
He names each sight out loud. A rust-and-scarlet tractor

far off ticks and ticks,
iambic, almost English, up and down.
He scans a leather-bound hillside, patiently unzipped

in long crumbling lines
that speak to him: 'homewards'...'plod...'
they say dimly. Or the lea. Even 'God', for the rhyme,

but 'zipstich...?'
Do the seagulls, like smoke rising
in the tractor's wake, really 'cleek'? With a twitch

he's awake. Beside
his bed, the youngest daughter bends,
as if reading him, all his strangeness writ large in her eyes.

'You brought me back'
(How can he say it?) 'I was miles away.'
(Her eyebrows quirk.) 'Tractor? You know? Trak trak...?'

He mimes the up, down,
up of it. 'Cut wheat? Zipsticher? No?'
She is backing away, her blue eyes darkening to brown.

'Zyvrosht!' Said,
done. She sparkles, runs, returns
triumphant, all the family with her, and a slice of bread.

House of Paper

A low table. Two cushions. Two
cups set. And no one here but me

in a room with no walls,
only thin paper screens,

paper screens beyond screens
hung from ceiling to floor. Light

moves in and is moved among them
from I don't know where.

If I'm the guest
I'm unannounced or uninvited.

Say I'm the host...?
As if a door opened somewhere

a rustling spreads. Almost
a whisper. I can almost hear.

4

THE SON OF
THE DUKE OF NOWHERE

(1987-91)

Welcome to the Forest
(for HD, at 36)

So here it is: the walled-up door
    only visible at certain
shifts of light, the door the stories
    mentioned. Now it opens
for you; one step and you're somewhere

else. That cats-and-cabbage smell,
    the murk, the sinking
underfoot, the rising damp you feel
    in your bones say: this is
it, not a figure of speech, this is all

the forest there is. Here's an armchair
    unbuttoned like Falstaff,
a snakepit of bedsprings, some lovers'
    burst balloon, a single
small red welly and a dumped Cortina

drifted deep in leaf-mould. You're just
    passing through? That's
what they all said. And you're almost
    sure of the path until
it twists again. And whom do you trust:

the woodman whistling through his teeth
    as he buffs up his axe?
Or the wolf-boy who comes sidling out
    to lay a clutch of pignuts
and a snared thrush dumbly at your feet?

Away From It All

He tried to write home
again, then crunched in the mist down the shingle,
out past the pillbox burying itself backwards

like a crab. He went stooped
as if hunting the one perfect globe of a stone
that must exist somewhere. The sea got up uncombed

with a scurf of rusty scud
and polystyrene. He was listening for the stream
that would burst up through the pebbles with a roar

come Spring, the locals said.
Even they had been making themselves scarcer
like the hours of daylight. The only trace

of any other life was the mould
on the mixed-fruit jam, *Five Go To Devil's Island*
and a book of crosswords, half-done, wrong.

The gas had puttered out
days since with a whiff of fish. He lay in silence
scoured by the all-night traffic of the waves

and woke to a shudder of flight,
was it, once, overhead, then the flat wonk
of a goose come adrift from its squadron.

He had wanted to write
'I'm as free as the wind here, nothing to distract
me from...from...'The paper stayed as blank

as the mist that shifted blind
on blind, and suddenly was alive with nothing
he could see: a quivering hum, a slap of tackle,

whickering taut wires...
A flock of white sails beat by, white-blind,
feeling their way home along the shore.

Son of Snotnose

tattnina (Estonian): a small oil lamp, literally 'snotnose'

There's a smutty flicker
on two crescent faces:
one, a woman hauled up
in her ninth month; one, a maid
who fusses at the wick

that drips, drips.
'Stop your cackling, child!'
In the stung hush
something up the hillside
crackles and spits

like brushwood
catching fire. Now again
a lumbering crunch.
The flame jinks. Then
'It's stopped.' Across the yard

hens ruffle and subside.
'What now?' Drip
drip. They're still,
so still
that when the door kicks wide

it's he who hangs amazed,
the enemy, the uninvited
guest, swaying in
towards their light,
one fist half raised

but trembling, rifle
slung askew, that shallow
Tartar face... A boy,
half way to dead and knows it,
and how many miles

from home. No one
can move. He stares and stares
till the thud of a shell
rattles the shutters.
Then he ducks and runs.

A wrenched hinge creaks.
The squat flame trips
in the draught.
The snotnose drips.
When the woman speaks

it's a rusty whisper: 'Quick.
Get water. Wedge the door.
Help me.' It is 1919
and not much else is clear.
'And for God's sake trim that wick.'

The Duke of Nowhere

I was the son of the Duke of Nowhere.
Nowhere was home. The first sound I remember

was engines sawing steam, the butt
and squeal of waggons full of clunk

shunted cruelly. Lifted to the window sill
I had my first sight of our exile

as I thought: Here, me,
watching...There, trains, going away...

        *

He was living incognito
but his secret was safe with me.

I was the solitary heir to everything
he never once mentioned. I guessed

from his brooding, his whole silent days,
it must be vast. The lost estates

grew vaster in the weeks,
then months, he went away and stayed.

        *

Beyond the roofs, beyond the dockyard wall
were cranes, then the edge of the world.

On a clear day I could watch grey frigates
climb it and slip over. I woke one night

to singing in the streets that suddenly
grew small as all the hooters of the fleet

brawled up together, blurting
Home... as if any such place

existed, over the horizon, anywhere.

Lahti

1

...the child won't sleep,
does it to spite us, you'd think
there was no one in the whole world but him,

even when we're alone
what do we do but argue about him,
we never just sit and not talk now, we can't begin,

and that's without the endless
calling – 'Just this once...' – night
after night – 'I'll never ask again...' – the same lie,

we put a stop to that but now
he creeps, the child gets out and prowls,
just when we get quiet on the sofa there's a creak on the stairs,

that's why I keep the wireless on,
Light Programme, but I hear, I can't stop myself
listening, thinking Where is he now? God knows where it'll end...

2

There are no wolves in England.

Not on the landing
or the long downstairs.
Not in the kitchen

where the lino glistens
like dark ice.
Not in the yard

behind the toolshed
or the toilet door.
There's nothing

in the shadows of the trees
but shadows.
Everybody knows

the wolves are gone,
gone limping
off across the snow

so far from anywhere.
However many
there may seem to be

each one sits singly
and their howls
only lengthen the night between them.

3

It was built like a miniature Odeon
in wood veneer. It had a cheeky dial
that blushed when it was on. The grille
at the back showed valves that hummed

in their own dimmed cathedral glow.
Uncle Mac's Children's Favourites was OK
but when no one was looking I tuned to Lahti
and caught the sound of snow

or sometimes a faint howling. Night
after night I haunted the landing. A band
of warmth would glow under the door
I never could open. I thought they might

pick up the signal. But I was too far
north, in Lahti. They were in some private
south with Perry Como. Magic Moments,
he sang. Catch a Falling Star...

Saying When

Was it *then*, as we stopped by the river
watching our charmed blur shiver off downstream
towards the crushed sound of the weir?

Was it then that the world
became less than it was: she died,
in a room above deep gardens that grew wild

by night, the houses dark beyond, a postage stamp
of window lit maybe to frame
a single head, a lamp?

Was that when one more country became nowhere
on the map, with its cafes, its spas
weeping condensation, its grey commissionaires

in chocolate coats with stiff gold tassels?
Uniforms were innocent as plumage,
years piled lightly as the flakes of strudels

she force-fed guest...Those, and powdery
moon-shaped biscuits, sinister
with almonds. 'Let the boy eat!'

she would cry. She had a sweet decaying smell,
cut flowers. 'Let him eat while he can.
Who can tell?'

Was it then,
when all at once you shivered,
'Let's go home'? Or when

a haze off the river rose up like a swan
into our headlights? I swerved but it was nothing
and no sooner seen than gone.

Envoi
(for SMK – 11.9.88)

There was a high green after-sunset
like an empty picture-palace
dimming to a glow

before the main feature.
Nothing. Space.
And the hills folding in for the night

and a small plane
rising, an X-
marks-the-spot silhouette

that dissolved
between one glance and the next,
the wing lights moving on.

It was nothing to do with you,
no sign, no metaphor.
It was nothing beyond

itself: a small
plane rising as down in the dark
I watched and you

were dead. But for a moment
it seemed clear: there was space
to hold us. That was all.

I would have liked to tell you.

A Summit
(Slovenia, 1987)

Miles down, the Jesenice steelworks broils
but we find last year's snow still dossing
wrapped in pine-mess, a tramp in a sack.
The trees all wear hair shirts of lichen.
A cloud moves through the wood. Dull bells

of drop-eared sheep nod by. A cuckoo
mocks itself. Somewhere up in the mist
is a line where the mountains trade names
like small change. There's a frontier post
and peaked caps, but the cloud slips through.

In a roadside hut, the man behind the bar
pilots his radio dial to catch the news
in any of five languages. All are scrambled
by a sound like crumbling scree. Too
far above it all, our reception is poor.

Out in the woods, the ants are building empires,
ziggurats of dead wood, towers of Babel.
They only need a flagpole; I plant my stick.
Hundreds swarm up. At the top they wave
then blunder back, wagging antennae: Brothers,

turn back! There has been some mistake...

What the Mountain Saw

They arrive by night, travel-stunned, and see nothing.
They sleep wrapped in pine-tang and the rush of waters.
The father is first awake. He clacks the shutters back
and a mountain squats square at the window, looking in.

It never leaves them, though it changes hour by hour,
twisting a scarf of cloud, or turning a hard profile
to the morning sun, or dissembling a sugar-pink haze.
However far they walk – and they walk, walk every day –

it's above them, a bit of beyond. Some snow hangs on
in shreds. This is a famous north face, and a killer.
Each day the father scans it with his old binoculars
for any hint of tracks, and never finds them.

So the holiday proceeds, in a series of snapshots,
here, in mid-stride, he crests a rise, wife and child
at his boot-heels, tranced by their thud and the heat
and insect hum. But the snow-face is no nearer.

Here, through veils of spruce, he breaks into a glade
possessed by pallid green-veined hellebores.
Or here, he brings his family, breathless, to its knees
before one icicle-white wild crocus. Here is the lake

he finds them, like a souvenir, round and still
enough to hold the mountain, till a fish jumps.
In between, there are the hours he drives them on
for health. Stop too long, the sweat begins to chill.

'Breathe deep!' he cries, and strikes out higher
up a wide white stony stream bed, tumbled and scoured
by the spring melt, strewn with tree trunks, torn
and bleached, and a few tiny tough mauve flowers

he can't name. He grips the child's hand as she teeters
on a plank beneath a waterfall. Its ice breath touches them.
Their hair goes white with spray. Afterwards he will say
'That was our furthest point,' and sigh. As they drag home

footsore, the mountain shows itself again behind them
in its pure dream of itself, untouched…Just as now
it looks in through the breakfast-room window when the child,
as if the strings that control her had fouled

and were jerked tight, has one of her turns. An egg
tips from its silver cup, a glass pirouettes to the edge
but has not yet smashed, the other guests have not
yet turned to stare, the father reaches for her but

is frozen. He will never reach her. Any moment now
the yolk will burst on crisply laundered linen. Soon
there will be splinters and tears. Behind it all he sees
the mountain at the window. If one could stand there

looking down, he thinks, this would all be very small.

Petit Mal

Just a flutter
behind your eyes,
a swirl of snow

that melts at a touch
and you wonder why I ask
Where did you go?

What happened?
'Nothing,' you say.
It's nothing, true:

a tiny death?
a leaving home?
Who knows? Not you.

Not the feverish script
writ by the moving
finger of the EEG.

Not the maze-mandalas,
shadow-maps,
that are all I see

in the brain-scan
negatives. No trace
of the gusts of flight

or free fall
I've felt brush
past me to light

wing-quivering
on your skin, as if
to mark you out. So

slight. So hard
to hold you. Harder still
to let you go.

The Dancing Princesses

It was an age of ballgowns: antique whims
she dredged up barnacled with gems.

Day in, day out she drew them, her exquisite
dummies. How could they dance? Hands and feet

were afterthoughts. And their perfectly lovely
empty faces last of all, their eyes only

for her. Unfluttering, they stared her through
and through. They would not let her go

till they'd taken one year of her ten.
Then something hidden by the gowns began

to connect, hand to foot. To move, before
my eyes. To dance. We are not what we were.

No more king, no princesses…The last
of her line furls a billow of scarlet,

quick as something going up in flames.
And there, arm locked to her waist,

is a thin man, all in black,
stiff as a stake. His back

is to me. I can't see his face.

On the Hoof

Sweet musk
of sweat and chips and petrol.
Sunglassed cabin cruisers lie

at anchor like a sneer of perfect teeth.
The waves slope off
smudging fingerprints of diesel.

One last toddler pokes
in a pickle of weed
collecting bits of crab

to build one of his own and
Shark, mummy, shark!
A stiff

rubbery cosh
of a dogfish, ditched,
too small for sport or meat.

The child is smacked.
The gulls come sidling.

Now
the front lights up. I cruise
the menus. I approve

the mushroom quiche and salads
you and I might choose
together, then move down

to the Char-Grill Bar-B-Q.
I've got to eat
and fast. Tonight

two hundred miles from home
I feel like meat.

The Big Bang Disco flickers.
It's a heart
that suddenly begins to beat.

The lads are all edgy with style.
The girls wear hungry midriffs
bare this year. A bouncer

with a knuckleduster jawline
counts them in
and they're skittish but meek

to his touch: warm bodies,
shuffling feet,
nudging on down the narrowing chute

the way flesh does:
not grass, but meat.

107

Heavy Weather

Close. Close as undergrowth.
The air a sweaty animal
that rubbed up against us. Nudged
between us. Close. We tossed
side by side all night, waiting

for something to break. Couldn't touch
for the heat. Even the thunder
kept its distance. Limply
I offered a joke: 'the drums,
the drums...' But you were asleep.

Or pretending. Teasy spats of rain
came and went and couldn't
clear the air. We woke exhausted.
Peeled on clothes that felt rubbery-
damp. Thought: Now what? Went our ways.

＊

    The weather does it. All at once
all over town, cracks in pavements, patios and walls

    boiled over: a thin greasy froth of wings.
The ants rose groggily, fumbling each other in flight,

    each pair a fantastical flying machine
of sex that came crashing down. The neuter groundcrew

    scrambled. I knelt to watch one queen
on our doorstep, dragging her slim spent male

    in the wake of her chariot, still coupled.
They had begun dismantling him. One clutched a wing

    overhead in the scrum, like a papery fan
or a dubious bargain from a jumble sale.

An Incident on the Line

(near Dawlish)

It's the same wet week, the length of England.
Each glistening station-stop depletes a few

till just three of us loll – half doze, half daze.
We've left our faces unattended. A cardboard cup

has been rolling to and fro, tick
tock, since Taunton. There's a thin girl opposite

who sits so tight, the cords of her throat
make an angle with her collarbones.

Her magazine stays shut. She bites her lip
in her sleep; in sleep, her man expands,

his bare arm drapes her like a boa.
Fields of flood slip by where cows and swans

dip into their own reflections.
Dusk draws up mud flats like velvet drapes

to part them in one swish: night
laced with grapplings of foam. Spray

jounces along the sea wall; a slap of it
smacks the window, combs itself away

in kite-tails, bright milky shudderings.
The slumped man grunts; he shifts his weight

on the girl. Her eyes open – she's not slept –
to stare over his head, out, where the next

wave bunches and swings for us.
She's learning not to flinch. At no one

I can see, she almost smiles.

Dust

Here they come, made of books, made of skin,
    dancing into the breach
between us. They're common as dirt: the least

subspecies of the order Angel. Poor things.
    Sunlight uplifts them.
All they want to do is drift and praise

but we bother the air
    with our clinches and tiffs like electrical storms.
See how they twitch.

Now I sit and will them: peace, be still.
    Your mug of cooling tea
gives up its ghosts. The door slams; bright

concentric ripples run
    into, and shudder through, each other's arms.
How do weightless

creatures mate? Just now, frisking a cobweb
    idly I brought down
on my head a slow crumbling cloud.

On its crest something stiff
    and silvered surfed at me: the bodiless
leg-chassis of a spider.

As I flinched, it followed, drawn
    by more than gravity –
the clutch of an old woman in the crowd

with something she just has to tell me.

The Way We Are
(for H.G.)

1

No secrets. Half our lives
together now...There's nothing between us
   left unsaid, nothing except...

   I can't say. If I could
I would pen you a flawless poem, of no lines,
   only spaces. This isn't it.

2

   A purple flush, almost
a weed... It's not till it stiffens
   and parches, going to seed,

   that we prize it. tastefully
arranged. Its inscrutable ricepaper face,
   snuffed lanterns, tethered kites

   fret in a draught too slight
for us to feel, with an itchy sound.
   Dry, everlasting. Honesty.

3

   So here we are, as if
we had climbed and climbed, on a twisting
   and backsliding scree track, up

   through hours of mist
to stop
   and stand together

   at what might be
a crumbling drop – no guide, no view
   and not a word to say.

4

There's a structural fault. Surveyors
frown: 'I'd have built somewhere else if I was you.'
    Cracks, hairline fractures everywhere

    – in the tired skin of our eyelids,
in the concrete of the yard where the children
    do studious hopscotch (step on a line

    you're out!) while on the threshold
of another year I hesitate, with this dried bouquet
    and a modest proposal: shall we go on?

5

We've plastered it, we've bodged. It opens new each year,
    a fine lightning track, ceiling to floor.
        It has become familiar

as these creases in our palms, that fork and stutter
    and get crossed; strange voices *will* cut in,
        bills, children, other

calls on our time, squalls of interference. Then
    we hold this old crackling line of pain.
        It connects us again.

6

    And if the crash comes? I expect
    to meet you in the rubble, half a brick
in hand. Here's mine. Together we can build a crack...

Big Wheel

I touched your hips; I felt your skeleton.
    My finger bones

cupped the hinge of a thigh, the nub of it, so little
    flesh between.

And there I was, in some museum, face to face
    with an exhibit, 'Human

Female and Infant' – the clean crib of her pelvis
    empty and the oh-

so-narrow exit and the baby's cracked-egg dome,
    a perfect fit.
                    And I couldn't let go

like our fling together on the big wheel. Caged
    in cheap thrills

and girders and 100-watt bulbs, the kids screamed
    tirelessly. We watched them

reeling off, weak-kneed, falling into each other's arms.
    Twice their age,

we dared each other to it. The man clinked us in
    without smiling. Threw the switch.

Heavy metal pumped suddenly, swung us up
    in one snatch, juddered,

stopped. We hung in a groundswell of dazzle and dark:
    our big O glittering

its own advertisement across the night, with us, slung
    between creaking bolts, holding on for dear life.

A Crumb

As you paused to flick away
one crumb, all you'd been saying, all
I was about to say

deserted me. I saw the tired
skin – sand creased by a flash-flood
then parched – inside

your elbow, in that place
with no particular name. Erosion,
grain by grain...I can't make

you beautiful. It frightens me,
how little we miss, so close. Not a crumb.
What do you see

and not say, that I deceive myself I hide?

What love can't do
is save us from ourselves, or from each other.
All it can do is be true.

5

THE END OF
THE PIER SHOW

Catch

Here is a woman. Here is a man.
And here is how the game began.
We call it Catch Me If You Can.

He was the one and only.
    She wrapped him all around.
He kicked against his swaddlings.
    She knew where he was bound
His first cry was 'Ergo Sum.' She knew the proof was sound.

I play Robber. You play Cop.
We play Catch You On The Hop.

He toyed with a naked razor.
    She taught him how to shave.
He said: I'm off to do or die.
    She waited like the grave.
He left her on the harbour wall and she became a wave.

I play Therefore. You play If.
We play Try To Catch My Drift.

He was the lost explorer.
    She was his New Found Land.
He was the pilgrim father.
    She was the shifting sand.
She was the straw he clutched at when he'd nowhere left to stand.

I play Sorry. You play Scold.
We play Couldn't Catch A Cold.

He mused in a country churchyard.
    She was the tongue of the bell.
He prayed to become a hermit.
    She was his spidery cell.
When Heaven left him cold in bed, she was the fires of Hell.

I play Day. You play Night.
We play Catch My Bones Alight.

He ran away to battle.
  She met him dressed in red.
He won a famous victory.
  She was the wound that bled
and out of it marched the living and into it marched the dead
and there was nothing he could do and no more to be said.

Here is a woman, here is a man
and they are nowhere.
Peace at last...?
                    But

Is that you?
                    Yes. Is that you?
Can we begin again?
                    We can.

from A Game of Henge
(for John Eaves)

1

A game of Henge, my masters?
The pieces are set. We lost the box
with the instructions years ago.

Do you see Hangman? Or
Clock Patience? Building bricks
the gods grew out of? Dominoes?

It's your move. You're in the ring
of the hills, of the stones, of the walls
of your skull. You want to go?

You want out? Good – that's
the game. Whichever way you turn
are doors. Choose. Step through, so...

And whichever world you stumble into
will be different from all the others, only
what *they* might have been,
                    you'll never know.

2

Those stony backs. A scrum around a whisper:
  Hush. Hiss. Who?
Why won't they let you in? No, it's a
  secret   secret
  won't tell YOU...

A playground wide as Wessex. Wire barbs
  the wind whines through.
You'd wait a hundred years and couldn't ask.
  It's secret   secret
  won't tell YOU.

Don't dare. You dare yourself to dare
  and then you do.
They turn and...What's the game? *You* are.
  And it's *Sticks And Stones*
  and you're on your own
  and it's Piggy In The Middle
  and the piggy is YOU.

3

It wasn't so much the stones
I loved, aged nine.
It was the word *archaeology*.

It was books pocked with diagrams
like pawprints round the bins
in last night's snow;

they showed circles complete
with the things that weren't there:
post holes, lost stones...

like the scene of the crime,
the victim's parting gesture
plotted on the pavement,

or the files the dentist kept on me
and everyone, living and dead
cheek by jowl in his metal safe.

Like the shudder and thrill
when I read in the paper:
'They identified him by his teeth.'

4

We're back to back
in a circle of stones

like a stopped clock,
gap-toothed cogs,

and whatever's the time
we can't tell any more

than the face knows
what it's showing.

If the sky can see
what figure our two bodies

make together it's not letting on.
I don't want to turn,

one more click of the ratchet.
If we could hold perfectly still...

But the sun and stars and other
working parts work on. A grain

of quartz winks with its perfect timing.
We can't see the shadows move;

they will touch one of us before the other
no matter how close we huddle,

equally afraid
it might be me, it might be you.

5

They've left their imprints in the rain
    even larger than they were
        as if the stones
had been whistled off, called home
    to lie down with their masters
        and there's only
their shadows left standing, hugely
    patient but shuffling slightly
        – or is it just
flurries and gusts of the rain? They shift
    from foot to foot like the queue
        for the very last bus.

6

Now you see them... Now you don't.
    The more you think you see, the more you stare.
    The more the shutter clicks, the less they're there.
        The final trick!

We'll need several thousand volunteers.
A million tons of concrete.

Cast a bald and bare
sarcophagus and seal them deep,

safe as nuclear waste.
Let there be steps like an Aztec pyramid

and on the top a pyre
to which processions of the unemployed

will bring every photograph and postcard,
all the evidence. A tourist guide or two

will be sacrificed (with simultaneous translation).
It will be dreadful. It will be taboo.

Then let the rumours begin. A hint. A joke
in poor taste. Let there be dubious

old men at dusk nudging over the mound
with their hazel twigs twitching. And in bus-

shelters and bike sheds let young whispers start.
The true Stonehenge will rise

again, story by story, faithfully
restored in all its glory:
                              whopping lies.

Frost Fair

    fires on the ice
    tonight's the night
for fighting cock and baited bull and dancing bear
    men swallowing swords
    and tugs of war
and everyone who's anyone is there

we're talking entertainment now we're talking the big show
we're talking tricks and treats we're talking kicks
we're talking the Now scene talking like there's no tomorrow
we're talking pleasure cruises on the River Styx

    fires on the ice
    tonight's the night
there's everything to sell and none to spare
    and everything's more
    than we can afford
we'll blow the lot tonight and we won't care

we're talking business now we're talking the big deal
we're talking quick bucks talking Futures talking Gilts
we're talking Big Bang talking big risks talking the Big Wheel
we're talking greasy poles and dwarves on stilts

    fires on the ice
    tonight's the night
for preachers peddling their whys and wares
    the hangman's drop
    and whip the top
the dark beyond the fire, the hungry stares

we're talking bigshots bigwigs talking pride before the fall
we're talking tightrope walkers strongmen quacks
we're talking walking on the water talking anything at all
we're talking hopscotch don't step on the cracks

   fires on the ice
   tonight's the night
there's red smoke rising in the glassy air
   the ice may creak
   beneath our feet
we'll dance with frost and ashes in our hair

Enter a Poet

So there they were,
tête-à-tête with a candle.
Could it be...? Yes,

Truth and Beauty!
They were just like in the pictures,
in profile, at least.

They were deep in each other's eyes.
He was drinking her in:
'But darling, you're so

beautiful!' She clinked
his glass: 'Oh
darling, you're so *true*...'

That's when they noticed me.
'Mind if I join you?'
Beauty's face set in a scowl;

Truth muttered, 'Actually
we were just leaving.'
The candle went out, too.

The Tale of 'You' and 'I'

Je est un autre.
RIMBAUD

If 'I' is another
then who is this lover
called 'You', this soul-mate, shadow-mother?
    Let's play I-spy
    on 'You' and 'I'
as they meet by the winding and whispering Wye.
    It's a strange affair
    as we follow them there
to a shifty hotel in the back streets of Ware.
    We're quick to spot
    them (too casually) jot
in the guest book: 'Mr and Mrs Watt.'
    How who touches whom
    in that inner room
depends on the guilts that we presume
    and innocence
    is no defence
against the eavesdropping of Whither & Whence
    (our private eyes
    hired to surprise
the naked truth in this tissue of lies).
    We burst the door
    but find no more
than quotation marks strewn on the floor.
    Our birds have flown.
    We're on our own
but the doubts conceived that night have grown
    into waifs and strays
    who dog our days
with their questionmark claws and wise-child gaze,
    whom we can't shoo,
    who will always pursue
the 'You' in me...the 'I' in you...

Wednesday's Child

Washed up on the shores of Wednesday
the nearly new lamp stand sat
    in a puddle of gloom
    in an empty room
in its pink silk tasselled hat.

And no one had bothered to tell him
when the time of day went past.
    She'd been tempted to knock
    but the grandfather clock
had told her to run on home fast.

And the door bell might have mentioned
but his batteries were flat as the floor.
    He could only speak
    with a whispery creak.
The knocker hung limp on the door.

The lace curtains twitched at her passing.
The bluebottles fussed at the pane
    and failing to grasp
    the idea of glass
died of thirst within sight of the rain.

But I'm telling this story on Monday
and honestly, none of it's true
    and I swear that the guy
    who could tell such a lie
isn't me, and not thinking not thinking not thinking
    not me and not thinking of you.

Secret Garden

Round and round the garden
like a Teddy bear
one steptwo step
fall into a snare

mummy's making mantraps
daddy stays away
watch your step
that's what bears say

daddy's gone a-hunting
bought a rabbit skin
bloody on the inside
to wrap his baby in

hiding in the brambles
no one knows we're there
don't start crying
stupid bear

round and round the garden
year on year on year
keep mum   stay dumb
hurting under here

who locked the gate
who threw away the key
who hears the growls
of the bear that prowls
round and round and round the garden
        inside me?

Shift

In the city of No
it's one way, lights at Stop or Caution; peristalsis in the belly of the beast
makes traffic flow...
   Move on

through the precincts of Nor
past coffee shops where ladies of a certain age meet lives they never had,
comparing what they never wore.
   Move on

down the high street of Nope
past street-squatters in battle fatigues, with inflammable eyes, with lean dogs
given just enough rope.
   Move on

round the ring road of Nay.
Billposters flense a huge grin, barbers mowing lines of shaving foam and skin
that falls like tickertape.
   Move on

past the dockside at Null.
Bags, drowned fish, condoms, years float by beneath the mugger's eye, the rag
and bone cry, of the blackback gull.
   Move on, move on.

In the poolhalls of Nil
a lean lad stretches like a leopard out along his cue. Crunch of the balls like
the bones of the kill.
   Move on.

When the city of No
shuts one eye for the night, with a sound of trouble breathing, when a sudden
doorway steams as if it's all about to blow

don't wait to be told.
   Just go.

Grace Notes

1

Play it again...
Sure thing ma'am.
I'll unzip a grin six octaves wide.

See me tickle those ivories
till they hurt. See me rinsing my fingers
in palpable hit. As time goes by

the soundtrack spits and lurches
out of sync. The keyboard ripples
like oiled pectorals while I

(won't you bend close and whisper
the words in my ear?) mime.
See me mug and smile.

2

Two one-man bands
set their pitches on opposite pavements.
Two males of the species
    they glare.

One, harmonica wired
to his head like a chrome grin,
kazoo like a fly's snout,
    shifts his feet

with the champ of a cymbal.
Both their drums palpitate.
They advance towards each other
    slowly. Silence

rings the spot where they are bound to meet.

3

The girl with the Walkman
screws her eyelids shut

as if to keep the sound in.
Bass rattles her bones;

the treble leaks out
like the sweeping up of crockery

when the couple upstairs
have had one of their tiffs.

(When they make it up later
in their rusty bed

it's like a woodwork-
for-beginners class

knocking up a pig pen
with a pig already in it.)

4

How-could-you-do-this-
to-me eyes, jowls like a threadbare sofa,
    the waiter looked round

    and seeing no one
in the place but us, and us snug
    in our corner of evening

    as if it was home,
sat down to nurse a mandolin
    no bigger than a ladle,

    tweaked a plectrum
from behind his ear, bent close
    as if threading a needle

    and began to quiver.
His sackfuls of shoulders, his thighs
    on the edge of his stool,

the chinks of light
in empty glasses, all went tremolo
   around the still point

of his plastic plectrum.
We didn't have the heart to ask
   for our bill. Remember?

Maybe you don't.
Maybe it wasn't you. The place
   closed three weeks later.

5

Saved from the grindstone round
of fairgrounds, Mister Mephisto's
   Mighty Musical Machine

needs a home. Someone to lag
his pipes and not mind when his breath
   comes short, to clean

behind panels where wires knot and rust,
stops glottal on and off and rotted
   valves squit steam,

someone, impossibly, old enough
to have bucked on gilded horses, young enough
   to believe they might be what they seem.

6

The Human Body, Illustrated –
that was one to read beneath the sheets.

I never reached the rude bits.
I got stuck on diagrams
that flayed us page by page:

the wetsuit of muscles, the veins
like cracks and creepers on a folly,
the worm-casts of gut

and the taut strings of nerves,
this twangling instrument
that's all I've got

to serenade you, like a café gypsy
with no violin
but the bared cords of his arm

as he bobs to your table.
Carves his bow. *Madame
wants music?* The cadenza

winces into, is it
love? as if it was the one sure thing.

The Song of the House

Who'll take these rooms, who'll rake the cinders in my hearth
    the house said, who can fill me?
I, said the tongue of flame, I'll lick you into shape.
No, said the house, your kind of love would kill me.

I, said the wind, just leave a little pane
    unlocked, I'll air you through,
I'll blow your memories away. No, said the house,
you'd leave me with no thoughts but thoughts of you.

I, said the rain, I'll stroke you, skin to skin,
    I'll treat you to a grey bouquet
of mould in every room, I'll weep with every crack.
No, said the house, you'd leach my strength away.

I, said the earth, I've waited, waited, wooing you
    with gravity, a love as true as lead,
let go and let me hold you. No, said the house,
nobody gets up smiling from your bed.

And then the emptiness walked in, without a word,
    and later we moved in, love, you and I.
There's this place in each other we can't have
or hold: uncurtained windows, hoards of sky.

The End of the End of the Pier Show

Undressing alone
in a room he won't remember
he's joggling on one leg

trying to kick crumpled jeans
like a slobbery dog
away. They won't let go,

then drop and won't
lie down, but keep the form
of crotch and thigh,

still warm, as if
he'd peeled himself off neatly.
Skin. Face. Smile.

It's the end of the show
and in some back-
stage hole

a mirror
framed in bare bulbs stares
across the dressing table, blank

as a poker fiend's face.
The name on the posters
has let himself out

by the back way
locking up behind. Beneath
the planks beneath his feet

foam sucks on girders.
Anglers hunched in a row
don't turn as he passes,

punters queuing all night for a show
that's already sold out
and no one told them .

At the passport-photo booth
he tries the slot
out of habit, just in case

there's a face to spare.
He frisks himself
for 10p. There's always his friend

for a moment like this –
the ghost, his friend
the ghost in the Speak Your Weight machine.

6
I.D.
(1991-94)

Nocturne with Glue

Listen, it's almost
not a sound at all –
the sound of 1 a.m.
It's peaceful
as the glaze of water
idling
just above the waterfall.

Somebody jets by
with his sun roof open
to the dark. He leaves a trail
of disco funk
like broken glass. I just know
he'll have a sticker: HONK
IF YOU HAD IT LAST NIGHT.

The binbags are out
sleeping rough again,
one with its mouth wide open.
A thin finicky fox
looks up
from its spillage of takeaway cartons.
It spares half a glance for me,

half for the thin boy
by the bus stop going nowhere.
He droops with the weight
of his head in his hands. He sways
as if combing the gutter
for something he lost but
what? He jerks round

with a whimpering growl,
he crouches, he snuffs deep
from his polythene bag.
It's a crumpled ego, a speech-
bubble saying Waitrose.
The fox shifts gear
smoothly, into fight-or-flight.

Flit

Black cab under the arches
ticking, lights killed,
engine drumming its fingers,
sparks flicked from the driver's
window like a lit fuse.
Black cab under hire

with its meter alive
like a sanctuary lamp:
red numbers twitch
in their sleep like dogs;
at after-midnight rates
they dream quick. I'm waiting

to see someone emptied on the street
in a downpour of send-offs
like the last New Year's Eve
of the century. Or creep
downstairs with one
case, the click of the latch

a loaded gun
cocked at too many years
of silence. I'm still waiting.
Is he out already
in the back seat of the black cab
clinching deals of love or money

or alone with the thrill
of watching time tot up
to the last p?
Then he'll tap the glass
and shake his wallet empty
and be gone. Black cab,

are you waiting for me?

Late

Someone was missing from my party.
I couldn't see who

as I slipped between everyone's glances
like a ladder through a stocking, through

to the back door and a breath of cold,

blind for a moment, then
in the crook of the crab-tree

a shiver of twigs, a thin-limbed
watchful child; it was me

looking back for a moment

then away
to where the plank gate

winced on a hinge somebody
should have fixed, into the lane

where I wasn't to go alone.

The Tennis Court in Winter

Between T-section stakes
set in puddles of concrete
the ten-foot wire-knit fence breed spikes
of crystal fine as root hairs
that feed off the air.

Just a point on the gauge:
in too quiet a dawn
we wake to find a revolution happened overnight.
Now the simplest of things,
our faithful unassuming

water, has become fanatical,
pure as Robespierre,
a stickler for a million points of detail.
This tarmac pound
becomes a parade ground

not yet trodden or a yard
where anybody serving time
might raise their eyes to see the wire barbed
with brilliance, a moment, blind
to what, if anything's, beyond

Beyonders

They live like us,
amongst us. Think of the years
they watched our houselights
from a distance. Now they're here,

they'll always leave 40 watts wasting
on the stairwell, or an anglepoise
downcast on the desk at midnight.
It's the same with their eyes:

you can see the bare filament
quivering, you can hear the brittle whine
like one mosquito in a lampshade
that puts them in mind

of the millions more that rise
out of swamp pools in veils
of cheap nylon that snag on your skin.
For a moment they're back

in the old beyond. Then
Sorry, they'll say
a bit too casually.
I *was miles away*…

*

They speak like us but
as if schooled in it later in life.
Their mother tongue is silence

only, when it falls,
each looks away.
Every one has a different dialect;

how can they hope
to reconstruct the histories they need?
Of a land where someone's ancestors

thrashed their grey herds to and fro
beneath the skirts of mother Winter
ducking most of her wallops.

Of a thousand-mile
branch line leading nowhere
but a barbed wire gate. Of days

chunked from the frost
and thawed by body heat.
(They have cold burns to prove it.)

Of some millennial
construction project sinking into bog
as steadily as it grows.

All lies. Besides
they never speak of it.
Don't ask me how I know.

*

What won't they do
for a bit of your warm regard?

They'll take any amount
and mail it home

except there's no address
and no one there

to take it in,
not now or ever.

*

Heard the one about the Boy
Lost In The Snow?
Ask any of them. They'll tell you.
Winter granted him one gift:
he could not die, or grow.

His tale dogged them to the city.
He could be roughing it out there now.
That could be his shadow
on any curtain, no matter
how carefully closed.

'How sad,' you'll say,
polite. They'll snort:
'The little bastard.
Once let him in
and you'll never be warm again.
        But a good story, no?'

                        *

Some sit it out
in bedsits. Most assimilate
hungrily. Some of them excel
in the art of forgetting till not
even they can tell
themselves from you or me.

I knew one who would sparkle and glow
at all the best addresses. Only,
when the last guest left,
the hostess found her carpet printed
with a cross-pattern tread of mud and snow

and nothing she could do would shift it.

Cut, Cut

The programme's in the can. That's me, cut clean.
Forget the out-takes tangling in the bin
like the mating of worms. Forget them, the dumb-
struck, the stumbles, a night-shelter full, like the hum
after the Late News, Shipping Forecast, Close Down...
    Quick, tune
me to another channel, easy listening, where a non-
stop DJ is driving his studio through till dawn
till his lights clip a hitchhiker miles from nowhere
mouthing things at the dark, but he won't pull over,
would you? Would you wind the window down –
    hey, kid, jump in?

Closed Circuit

Dead space: a lobby like the one
blank tank in the aquarium
there's always someone staring into.
   Buff peels from the wall

like hothouse petals, drab exotica
that pick themselves for any stranger.
There's the camera, bolted out of reach.
   Who's to know if that's you

swimming right now in a goldfish bowl
in someone somewhere's rank of monitors;
if they're yawning or tapping a roll-up;
   if they're there at all,

or if you're being reeled straight into canisters
to be date-coded, sealed and stored,
wiped in a week or held on suspicion
   in a matrix like the mind of God?

Hard Luck Café

It's always open. From inside
the sign on the door says CLOSED at all hours.
The old girl knows me at a glance.

She snorts a slow espresso
like a thimbleful of cobwebs
and nods in that know-something way

I'm beginning to hate just like one of the family.
'How's things?' 'Can't complain.'
Our words hang, turning slowly in the dust-light

like something a spider was saving for Christmas.
Old chess buffs,
we play out an endgame of empty cups.

In its cold violet glow
the Insect-O-Cutor spits and spits.
A daddy-long-legs shrivels on its grille.

Downhometown

(Delabole)

Houses littered down the roadside
like some lorry's shed load.

Here's where it's at, without the option.
Stacked blue plastic crates

glimpsed through the window
of the British Legion Hall.

Last weekend's fête,
a buff handbill slapped up

like an order to evict.
On the forecourt of the shut-up shop

the odd half dozen scuff their heels.
One stares up the road, then down

and can't decide. One considers the kerb,
leans his weight on a lamppost

and kicks the place as if it's jammed;
if he could just dislodge it everything

would light up and start humming.
The girls have memories already;

they name names from school,
who's in the army, who's in jail.

'What, Gavin? Him?' – 'The quiet ones,
they're the worst.' They stop

as if I'm nothing, passing,
but a slight chill in the air.

They don't look at each other but,
together, at the place I might have been.

Figure in Landscape: China Clay

A Desert Father might have been at home here:
acres of quartz slag that give to the boot
    with a masculine crunch.
    The soft stuff's gone,
pulled in grey-silky bolts, folded neat
in square settling-ponds down the valley.

No end to it: the moorside overflows
with grit cleanly as caustic soda,
    like the top hat
    plundered by a conjuror
with both hands shovelling a froth
of doves up, half-frightening, white as this

or the light of the mind. It's a Zen
monk's garden with one boulder left
   in rigorous asymmetry,
   the texture of fudge
made with ground glass, and concentric
ruts of tyre treads raked around it.

There's a breathing, like surf at the brink
of things, quite close, rising, falling and yes
   here's a fifty-foot gulch
   and a sandblast of spray.
A swivel-cannon with a throbbing hose,
way down, is stropped to piss the cliff away

while in his sentry box one living soul
sits his shift out. Swills of froth
   make deltas round him.
   He might be a deserter
from the family this Bank Holiday, a father
for whom this place has come to seem like home.

He Went That Way

A shotgun cartridge
stomped in the rutted-up mud

it's not. It's a throwaway
flick-lighter, out of gas.

Zigzag tyre treads
have snarled up the verge

as if the whole damn lay-by
couldn't hold a man like him,

whoever he was, out of sight
up the road now, out of mind.

He'll be talking to thin air
signing himself on as Fozzie Bear,

143

locking in to anyone
who's passing on his wavelength

like a non-stop chat show
or a seance. He's a greyish haze

where the road impacts on a horizon
as straight-down-the-line

as a government health warning.
If this place remembers him

it's as dust and a burnt smell
settling. Wagtails tap-

test the puddles for damage.
You can see the whole sky

in a dented hubcap
and the clouds are heavy bruising

working to the surface
slowly, slowly.

Quite what's happened,
it's too soon to say.

from The Wolfboy's Progress

'Good...boy...' the Professor says
'Good...' (with his back to the locked door)
'That's a good boy' –

a voice like the tug of a leash
that I might even learn to call 'kind'
one day.

*

The woods have gone slurried with rain on the window.
In here it's all straight lines and rules.

The Professor keeps a black and white world in a book.
He spells it out   T...R...E...E...

I look away.
He can't fool me.

*

On the red leather sofa
lolls the smug dog. I crouch on the floor,
the only one she doesn't bounce to.
She looks down,

down on me with those dim eyes
they call trusting. Her no-nonsense nose
is sharp as a sharpened pencil, always
testing.

*

Shredded blankets
make a nest.
Crud-flakes clothe
its nakedness.

Chews its hunger
bitter grub.
Kips on sore boards.
There's the rub.

Snarls at pity.
Dumb thing lies.
Gentle gaolers
damn your eyes!

*

The forest won't have me back. I think she's angry.
She wakes me up shivering with the word 'hungry'

on my lips, where before it was simply wanting
as constant as weather. Now I'm drawn to haunting

outskirts. They're so trusting, leaving curtains
open to the dark. They leave their gardens

free for any thing of night to yearn and stare
in at...whatever people do in there.

           *

A cat
shrugs itself off its bin,
with bad grace
leaves its pickings to me.
Upstairs a child chafes at a violin.

A door
swings, shaking light out
like a tablecloth.
A woman calls. Someone is wanted home.
No answer. I could run

into that life,
those thrilling ordinary
cooking smells, into
someone to be. And here I go
again, led by the nose.

           *

Trapped, home again, Professor, tail
between my legs. I'll lap the gruel
of each day in the classroom, fool
among fools who grunt and grope for words.
I'll lick the plate and ask for more. For you
I'll grow up hard though scarcely
straight or true.

           *

And I can sing –
words pulled on the string of a tune
like a toy, a wooden duck on wheels
that clacks and quacks.

Sheet music frightens me,
those five-wire fences little notes
get snagged and hang on,
twitching to get free.

I'll settle for Country and Western
all lonesome and prayery, with coyotes
and love, love. Oh gimme
that sweet cringe and whine.

*

So one day there's this girl neat
as a clutch of speckled eggs.
I won't break one, honest.
Though, oh, I could eat
her up, and her mummy and daddy,
her regular bedtimes.
They'd taste sweet,
dry but more-ish, like nougat.
It's only that granny
who gives me an old-fashioned look:
Young man, don't I know you
from somewhere? I make them a gift
of my teeth: my most terribly
charming smile.

*

Memo: get myself a minder
get myself an agent
get myself connections
and a damn good brief

make myself a name
carve a slice of the action
make myself a killing
land on my feet

find myself a sugar mama
doesn't ask questions
when I slink back in the morning
lies and feathers in my teeth

sharpen up my clause
and my wits and my pencil
get ready to pass sentence
I'll suspend their disbelief

                    *

If you could see me now,
Professor – man of letters
to my name. In short,
   I pass

the last test, don't I?
They attend, wine glasses
poised, as I recite
   my party piece.

In the ripple this girl
I'd made a note of turns
her long neck to her beau
   and whispers:

*Don't you think he's good
for a...* (reckoning without
my pricked ears) *Don't
   you think he's...*

          Good
          boy. Good boy.
          ...good.

Static

A rip of tiny lightning in a darkened room.
Her back's torque tensed to slip

a nylon sweater... How could he
not touch? The same random electricity

is jizzling on her skin and his.
Now it arcs, a whip-flick

like the moment they first spoke,
that sent him home stung, wondering

where he'd been hit,
like a witchfinder with his needle inch-

by-inching for the damned spot
on himself, inevitably finding it.

Digital

Prescribe me digitalis
when the heart beats faster
as with fancying you, or fear,

or the sight of time
dealt in a straight flush
on a watch that's not a face

but a rear-view mirror,
signs and white lines,
tracer flashes shortening away;

it's the bullet-proof glass
behind which the bank girl
licks her fingers,

strokes the wad and counts
me out. There's no tick
at the bedside these nights

but green stick figures
try out all
the postures one by one.

They're teaching us to see
ourselves as liquid crystal
like the grid of a city by night

seen from a mile up,
where streets come alive
at the click of a time-switch,

contact made, your finger-
tip against my thigh.
Outside,

quite close this time,
a siren dopplers by.

Bonfire Night

As they're dumped, so they lie.
She's a soggy-damp mattress,
all puckers and lumps. He's her guy

with a head full of paper. His sack-
cloth skin itches them both
and his finger twigs scratch

where she's tender. He's stiff
in all the wrong places. Whoosh
from next door's garden and a whiff

of cordite... Always out of sight,
those oohs and ahs. Strike, strike
a match. The bloody thing won't light.

Bodily Fluids

That's autopsy language.
It means you and me.

It means holding each other
carefully, at finger's length,

like tall flasks that might spill.
And what price now, that dream

where we meet like an incoming tide
at the river's mouth, salt

water tangling with sweet?
I think 'safe', and see sweat-

marked costas,
a tidewrack of discos and bars

where last night's love
is a specimen bagged on the beach;

and I think of the monk
who meditated on his body's

entrances and exits – nine,
each with its own secretion;

and of breath prints on the window
where we looked out at the rain;

and of a world where bodies heat
to melting but can't touch.

I think: we've got to think.
But not too much.

Night Doubles

On the outskirts of somewhere bypassed in the night
    there's a fridge-blue cube of floodlight

with a high wire fence to hold it in. Matched pairs
    in white kit flicker in the charmed square

like aquarium fish twitching up to a sifting
    of feed. Now they're still; women

menace the net. One man coils for the serve
    that springs them all. They have several

shadows each, that shrink in, then splinter away
    as they leap. Outside the game

tonight, I can't help gazing in. It jiggles us.
    We fall together, or apart, like dice.

from A Day at the Earth-house

> *Underneath one particular stone in the south-west quadrant were not only*
> *medieval pottery shards but the crushed skeleton of a barber-surgeon,*
> *complete with leather purse containing scissors, probe and money.*
> THE AVEBURY MONUMENTS: DOE HANDBOOK

Under the Stone

Dry bones. Here's enough for a finger
to crook, to poke. Or two.
Diggers, down on your knees
like a priest's flock to a relic

or a wife who tries to gather every
fragment of the crock
her man flung at the wall
as if she might piece their lives together.

Can these bones live?
Toothbrush them free
as if the lie of them
held all the clues: whose hand

might drop its pouch of tools
and throw itself open
like cards slapped down
the devil take it, win or lose.

Earthwork

    Like a splash
in a green pond baized with duckweed
that a child could run onto
    and drown

    ditch and bank
spread; trees, stones, houses
bob in the jolt of a shockwave
    like visible sound

    where it sank,
whatever, pitched in. And the ripples
spread till you can't tell them from
    encircling downs.

Long Barrow

Late sleepers in the earth-house,
the long bunker on the hill,

this can't be *you*, this depart-
ment store of bones, thighs racked

by size, this lego-set of vertebrae,
toe bone winked in an eye socket. No,

whatever was you has leached out
with your private juices, out and down

153

into stream into soil into grass into cow
into milk and into children's bones again

and of your finest feelings all we know
is that you ached. Arthritis. Ask the bones.

Silbury Hill

The long she of the downs
(Compared to her

the great flasher of Cerne and all
that white-horse sky-gymkhana

are the chalk scrawls of a pavement artist
before rain...) stirs in her sleep

or pretends for you, flexing so
the slope from hip to waist

or collarbone to nipple tip
is silk pegged in the wind,

skin alert to be touched,
half an ache. And the way

she seems to shift
as you walk deeper, opening a green

cleave in the snug of it,
a glimpse of this soft nub, lipped

in ground that sometimes
in a season darkens

to marsh, responding
to the mood swings of the moon.

Sarsens

Heathen knights, felled
full length in their armour,
face down on the hillside, still
they dream us harm.

Will's girl, out late,
let just the shadow of one
touch her ankle and the child she got
was born cold as a stone.
   We say: Bury them.
When a good man loses wife or cow
or strength the stones know why and how.
   We say: Bury them, bury them.

Don't breathe a word of them after
but be careful where you dig or plough.

Dating

Purple gobbets on the sarsen.
Birdshit dates us: elderberry season.
   At the burial site
ants' wings found in the lowest stratum
nail the death on August. Last
   month's mating flight.

Crack

I know my bones. Which snapped. Pain? No,
I was a blade of lightning snickersnacked

lifting her face from the dark of her life
and all the generations in the earth-house stacked

like turves, brief flares of wives and daughters
interlaid with men. As I turned, in the crack

of the stone door a cat couldn't tease through
I stuck. Wanting out. Wanting back.

155

Resurrections

And last the archaeologists, the resurrection men,
pose with their big-game bag: a stone
trussed, tractored, block-and-tackled up,

a great slave at an auction, hung with chains.
And in the pit? A sidelong flattened grin. Dry bones.
Facts? Only moderate height. Male.

Slight build. Neck fractured in several places.
Artefacts? Pouch, leather, with a metal probe,
scissors, 3 coins (dated *circa* 1300,

one of them French), some shards of pot nearby.

Scarcely a *Christian* burial.

The Barber Surgeon's Song

Here's one for my probe,
my prick of wit
to get under the skin,
my goad, my God,
what pouches have I
kept it in?

Here's two for my scissor-
legs' well oiled hinge
opening time and again
to cut through thou-shalt-knots,
too sharp I hope
to cause much pain.

Here's three for the coins
from here and there
I never did spend.
Two even, one odd.
The reckoning.
That's it. The end.

Ex

Gusting across, not waiting

for the lights, just one more
loose end of the working day

leaking home through the cracks
in the traffic, at six

already dark...Across, between
a humped Wimpey-jacketed back

hugging two carrier bags
from the off-licence

and a shock-mascara'd
teenage mum gone grey

in my headlights
(her buggy-bound astronaut

bumping down
to a breath of exhaust on his cheek)...

Across, not looking left or right
between the neon CHRIST

IS THE ANSWER on the shut
shop of the chapel

and the Asian minimarket
(the whole family gathered in

round the freezer, disputing,
their faces lit upwards

in Christmas-card glow)...
Stooping across, between

my bumper and the brake lights
of a transit van, not an arm's reach away

and turning for a moment,
square on and not seeing,

it was you –
pale, puffed, distracted

as if flickered up
by my dipped beam out of focus.

I was glad to see you cast a shadow.

Time Out

There's a curt breeze up.
A grainy whiteness
far out. One gull looking for its shadow
on a mile of sand. And you,
how strange, it's you.

White wrought iron chairs
are leaning, elbows on their tables.
All the parasols are down
but one. It hackles and slaps
above you. You're taking your ease

deep out of any season,
in that bleached-out frock,
arms bare,
leaning back like a lady of leisure.
You ought to be chilled to the bone.

To a life
spent doling cups of kindness!
Now you drink, disgracefully, alone
taking clear water straight on the rocks.
The glass sweats with the cold.

The wind is impatient.
It wants to sweep under your feet.
You won't be hurried now.
A newspaper peels itself page
by page, and every one is white.

What news? There's silence in it.

Guest of the Atlantic

Blame the state I'm in this morning on the waitress,
her and her surfer, all night in the other attic room.

I'd passed them on the stairs. Her landed merman,
he looked like someone come to do the plumbing, or his mate,

with a six-pack toolkit. Then it was the steady scrape
of his voice through the wall, hers demurring, just enough

to keep us all up. When at last my toothmug started
rattling on the basin, all the crying-out-loud

was his. Then, quite soon, running water in the pipes
that connected us. Then his snores. Was she there at all?

                    *

Somewhere down the line I dozed and I was dreaming
I was Cornwall, varicose with rivers, cramped
in an armlock of sea. I was a crumpled map

full of words that were me too, but what
did they mean: Praze-an-Beeble, Zelah, Perranzabuloe?
Then there was dawn picking holes in the curtains.

I woke numb all down one side. I tried not to move
as if I could put off what came next, the pain
that would sew my two halves back together,

pins-and-needles like the screel of rooftop gulls.

                    *

The surf was mixing concrete all night.
There's the beach, new-laid,
spoiled with footprints already.
The wind flaunts straight into the waves
which start to smoulder – overheating brakes
or a tyre in a skid. Hot fat

nearing flashpoint. The surfers are up.
Reduced to their own silhouettes
in wetsuits they range out along a swell,
cave-painted hunters, watchful less
of the prey, which is vicious but slow,
than each other. Who will strike the killing blow?

                    *

In black-and-white, trim-pinnied, she's serving again.
There's a coffee-dregs look in her eyes.
She drops two rounds of post
beside my breakfast in a silver toast rack:

c/o *The Atlantic Hotel. Please Forward.*
Hungry for a Missing You or two
I slit them then, to prove I'm a free man,
let them lie, and read the window:

waves rule thick smudge lines;
the surfers' heads are punctuation
with no words. They break all at once,
all but one. He's waiting, days,

nights, for the biggie, the one
with his name lettered through it
like rock, the one that – since Chaos
Theory's all we've got to go on –

could be stirring in the womb
of the Atlantic now, conceived
by the cough of an outboard motor
somewhere in the Gulf of Mexico.

Mermaid, Zennor Church

She's not coy,
slipping out of her scales.
She peels them down like tights

   just so far.
Where the first tweak of hair
might be, they ruck and cling.

   She shows herself
simply, like the highest mathematics,
an elegant paradox, QED

   in wood that's charred
as if fresh from the stake. Still,
the just-risen swell of her belly

   comes out whole.
It's smooth, worn smooth: I'm not
the only one who's had to touch

   and touch again,
a bit shy to be caught kneeling
by the granite altar. Squeamish, too:

   what if my fingers brushed
against the scar-grain of the face
that's gone? Those four straight slashes

   scored through breasts
and forehead, cheek and chin? Yes,
touch there. gently. Pray for something

   to begin to heal, in me.

A Dangerous Age

He lifts up her face and she lets him,
she lets him smooth it
like a finely rumpled sheet,

stroking out from the eyes,
their dusty corners, down the cheek,
easing ten years away

for a moment. Forking lifelines wait
in the grain of the skin
as if scribed by a 5H pencil.

Rub gently, rub hard; held to the light
the traces show.
It's a dangerous age.

No wonder our grandmothers taught us
to put it away
like their guests-only china

so fine it held shadows. Not old
but not young, these two
tread the cusp, a narrow bridge

without a handrail, breathing quick
from the risk like thinned air,
touching at a time like this

just to steady themselves,
for safety,
though they know there's no such thing.

Mispickel

Mispickel: arsenic ore, reprocessed from the waste of worked-out tin mines

Here's the man, stepping back into daylight.
There's the furnace with its burnt-stone breath.

The hand he holds out is a mitt that grips
and nothing else; he's swaddled up to the slot

where his eyes shift and blink. Now he breathes
almost free. Come payday, that's a bob or two

he'll not say no to. I should leave him
to the facts, statistics settling steady as the smoke

downwind: he won't make thirty. Leave him
to bare hands, a woman's; quick, her fingertips

unpick him. Unable to do for himself
he waits; she winds the graveclothes off him.

Strip by strip, skin reappears. He stands
as naked as a thing she's made

and will make, again and again.
His chest is white as cuttlebone,

with scant black hairs and small sores
that don't heal. Half-baked from the ovens,

he has only her to finish him,
quick, while he's back from the dead, on leave.

She rinses, twining fingers in the bowl,
flicking the drops off, while he watches

as if nothing but her touch could make him speak.

Rites and Passages.

1

Dead water. Swamp mist swabs away
both shores, so there's no *to* or *from*,
no sign the ferry's moving with its freight
of families, displaced, clutching small
belongings. Only the deaf-mute has none.
He grins at the wake his finger traces
in the water. Our reflections come undone.

2

Click, clack, yes-sir, our garden windmill-
mannikin snaps to attention (dabs of black
and red suggest a uniform) then abases himself
in a right-angled bow: up, down. The windvane
edges, angles, sensing power, undefined
and shifting, like true north...while him,
click, clack, he thinks he drives the wind.

3

Spuds of flint in the furrows
scratched across the grain of downland.
Not a tree for miles. This post
marks nothing but a mid-point:
owl-cacked, lichened, like a lost
god, where a hedge was grubbed up,
where our paths once crossed.

4

In Stone Street, in a room without a door,
without paint or plaster, in two
narrow beds (which are one bed sawed
in half and propped a little more
than an arm's reach apart) a sleepless
man, a woman. It's as they once swore:
they said *Nothing will come between us.*

5

Aaah! The barbarians hiss. A brand
sputters, punched into darkness
and the flames swarm hand over hand
up walls of ivy tangle. All our faces
burn. *Tear it down, down, down,* we bay.
The folly crumbling, its cry escapes
our throats. We chase ourselves away.

6

Long dunes. A salt marsh. A grey man
hauling driftwood feels the tremor
and stiffens upright. Spattering sand
and hooves they're on him, bareback,
stretched, gone in a shudder of speed.
He watches them diminish, then
he stoops again. He has a fire to feed.

7

It's their day, the children. See them glow
and crackle. They claw the bright wrappings
away to find masks: one Papuan, an *oh!*
of real teeth set in clay; one Aztec,
spiked with feather shafts; one Maori, mazy
spirals; one bronze, from Mycenae,
blind; some of no age…

8

Waves on the shingle, white on grey
and a grey-wash sky. Among the stones
we find this clasp, a twist of male
and female, naked long-backed bodies
twined in blackened silver. But of who
wrought the knot, who lost it, what
it held in place…no clue.

Out There

Now this comes back, from nowhere,
like an unsigned postcard: snow
on a hill that cold-shouldered the town,
and tracks, our tracks, not close

or quite parallel, edging together
at last in a wood,
a clearing like a room
with the blinds drawn and furniture draped.

There were ashes trodden into mud
like cooled volcano slurry,
someone's fire. A strand of smoke
spooled up like milk in water.

When I flushed a flame
from cover in the cinders
it was pale
as something born too soon.

It had been keeping for the night.
She stayed deep in the folds of her coat.
I turned to say 'We should be going...'
but, just for a moment,

could not think which way was home.

7

THE WASTING GAME

(1994-98)

Visiting Persephone

Can you picture *him*
going down to see her, fitting in
with the difficult visiting times?
He was her father, after all.

But to enter that dark,
that mould and mouldering, his power
and glory threatening to wink out
like a fused bulb with a pinging whine

would tax a better god than him.
She is yellowish pale this week
with a drained look, no pink
but some fresh scars on her arm,

the others aged to shrivelled plum.
She has keelhauled herself by inches
or been crawling down narrowing
ducts of slime and shale.

Some days she hardly greets him
and her silence is a waiting room
where he sits and is not called for,
feeling younger than she is, learning

to make out the shapes in her gloom.
The gifts he foisted on her
leave him dull, a Souza march
come shuffling to a halt

outside the darkened concert hall
where a child's violin
slips on difficult scales,
then you look and there's no one.

He gets up to go, go
where? How could he have imagined
he was any sort of god? How could he
have imagined this at all?

The Sick Child

(after Munch)

Looking down from the snowfields
of her pillow, she scarcely seems drawn,
rather, scratched on the skin

of the canvas till blood comes.
No, mother, she'll take nothing
from you now. Words least of all.

You brought her into this,
which leaves you at her mercy and
she's merciless. Head bowed, kneeling,

you're as faceless as a shadow thrown
by her face that's red-rimmed,
a house burning down,

fire staving out window after window,
up to the one where a child
about to be consumed

and knowing it, does not
call, cry, speak out of turn
or take her eyes off you

but is good, as always, gazing out
onto the wastes of childhood
like a rainy afternoon.

The Wasting Game

1

'I'm fat, look, *fat...*'

Yes and the moon's made of cheese,
that chunk she won't touch in the fridge

dried, creviced, sweating in its cold
like someone with a killing fever.

Half a scrape-of-marmite sandwich,
last night's pushed-aside

potatoes greying like a tramp's teeth,
crusts, crumbs are a danger to her,

so much orbiting space junk
that's weightless for only so long.

Burn it up on re-entry, burn it,
burn it. So she trains

with weights, she jogs, she runs
as if the sky were falling.

2

Curled like a lip, a crust dries in the bin,
the supermodel's come-on-don't-touch sneer
for the camera – desire
caught, teased, time and again

till all the wants run dry
and there's only this rictus,
a cat raking claws
down the arm of the chair,

eyes closed, lips apart
like the girl's head she drew
arching back to a lover's long
bone fingers tangled in her hair.

3

The eating thing:

the slouching beast
that's come to stay,

to spatter the slops
and foul the manger,

to snap at the hand
that tries to feed it, so

we leave it and we lie
in darkness, trying not to know,

not to hear it gnawing
in the next room, gnawing

itself to the bone.

4

Dry priestess at the shrine
of nothing. Maid-saint
fierce against the flesh
(burn it, burn it) denouncing
the witch in herself, see,
she's mounting the stake,
no, *becoming* it *and*
the tinder and the heartless
blaze you might mistake
for holiness. My homegrown
Manichee, almost 'perfected'
as the Cathars had it
fasting unto death. 'I want
a perfect figure.' Saying no
to the pull of the world.
Straight out, she said it
(burning but not yet
consumed) she said 'Weight
is bad. Bad.' On the blanket.
In the desert of her bed.

5

To be perfect...? 'Nothing's
perfect in this life,' I say.

Mealy middle-aged wisdom,

eat your words. See how
precisely she'll come to agree.

6

Close now, this nothing–

hungry thing that fills
her, that empties her... Once

in aquarium twilight a grey-
silver bass brought a face

big as mine up to the glass,
chewing water, with the weight

of deep ocean behind it. The cold.
Its tuppenny eye had a gleam

like contempt. For me? Or worse:
maybe its own reflection in the glass

was all it saw?

7

It's the Dark Ages now. I believe
in possession, in demons that speak
in crone voices out of fifteen-year-old lips,

her lips that have taken a tuck in
at the corner, a small crease like age
or disapproval when she (seldom) smiles.

I believe fairy tales like hot news,
how the Snow Queen's pinched
enraptured child might desire

nothing but to spell ETERNITY
from jags of ice, how Rumpelstiltskin
with the rage of any secret thing

that's named for what it is
might stamp so hard the splintering
could go on for ever,

how the scientists at Los Alamos
watched the fireball grow
and thought: it might not stop,

it might consume us all.

8

She's been paying her dues to gravity
in dud coin once a week

checking in on the doctor's scales
which wobble to a judgment: *holding steady*

though she's less and less able to hoist
what mass she still has, and she sways,

the rush of faintness in her ears like sea
hissing in over mud and in and in

as she steadies herself and walks towards it
with stones in her pockets, adding one a week.

9

Inside her, the slowing,
the faltering
voltage.
But still

there's this brilliant
flicker on the surface,
arc lights
on a dragged canal,

moving pictures
that don't quite
finesse the eye;
there are moments

you almost see through
(freeze *there*)
when the screen
shows nothing but a grey

room and gradually
shapes, near-transparent,
near-familiar,
like the threadbare home video

mailed with impossible demands.
You see the hostages,
a family,
staring out at you.

10

Ketones: a sour chemical smell on her skin
like a darkroom with blackouts on windows,
with shallow trays of fluid silky-still
as a swimming pool after lights-out,
their monochromes hardening. Developed,
they will close the family album.

11

I could hate

those frail maids fading beautifully
in books, wax lilies, pale-succulent

stalks that might snap
at a touch. The bird-dropping of blood

in a lace-bordered handkerchief
like the monstrance on the nuptial sheet.

A consummation most devoutly wished
by death. The maiden turns,

in woodcuts from another age
of plagues, to his knuckleboned touch,

half smiling; the consumptive turns
on her lace-bordered pillow

weakly and away
from any warmth of flesh

as if stung; the anorexic turns
her face towards these stories, stories

which, because I love the girl,
I hate.

12

She left home months ago.
Somehow we never noticed.
She was going solo

as a conjuror:
the egg we found rotting
in the body-folds of the sofa;

caked wads
of tissues in the bin with weetabix
compacted in them like the Mob's

car-crusher sandwiches;
potatoes spirited away
with one pass of the baggy-wristed

sweater she draped
on her bones. (What applause
when she whips it off one day

and she's gone!) Co-ordination
slipping now, caught out –
fraud, fraud! –

she plays the cheapest trick of all.
A toothmug of tap water,
sixty paracetamol.

She tries hissing herself offstage.

13

Drip. Drip.

Those stripped
twigs of her fingers.
Ivy torsions in the wrist.

Two spikes bandaged
to drip in her veins.

Sap sunk
at fifteen, she's been old
for too long, always cold
in her matt blacks, always
in some sort of mourning.

Mulched like leafmould,
mushroom-breathed, shit-smelling,
she's a question: Can
you love this?
Can you sit

and watch the hours dissolving
in the drip
of Parvolax and glucose
clear as rinsings from bare twig tips
when the downpour's gone?

They're trying to wash the river
in her blood. They're on the phone
to the Poisons Unit:
the readings aren't clear.
Nothing's perfect

but it's all there is.
This. Now. The drip
of plain words. Yes.
Love.
This.

Ledge

She's lodged here, somehow –
just a bed's width, dizzyingly high.

The mist pours up, sea clatters
trolleys in a lift shaft and their *why*...?

and *when you're better* are as clear
as a seal's cough and as odd. She could even reply

but she's using her time here to study the language of birds;
she's so light and hollow and her eye

so sharp that sometimes in the mist
she catches the glint of a zero-thickness steel wire cry

she could slip down and away, a miles-long glide.
Just a step to the edge and she'll fly.

Imago

She spent winter and spring
in her chrysalis, a strait world
shrunk and puckered like a mis-stitched scar.

Inside it held a breaking down of things
like a drop of original swamp sea.
Which is one way not to speak

of unopening windows resigned to the view
of the CAUTION PATIENTS CROSSING
speedbumped drive; the coded sign

NO CASUALTY DEPARTMENT here
among so many casualties;
the swabbed smells and the sounds off

like that sobbing on legs
down the corridor, and the dribbling
overspill from the padlocked pool

where a green beach ball scuds slow
eccentric orbits
to the pipe and back and round...

*

Hawk moth caterpillars
dropped from the limes in our street,
pointless manna she'd save

like the good girl she was,
on damp earth in a jam-jar.
They shrank to sealed flasks

for the usual great experiment.
We found a blood-brown drip
in the husk where one vanished;

another that, shrink-
wrapped too tight in itself,
couldn't ever split free.

So seeing her now
rise from the station subway
with bags marked for home,

to the lip of the crowd, and hesitate,
not a child now, and not any image
I could make to hold her,

I can't call her name,
I can't find words for her,
I wouldn't dare.

Trebizond

Some days nothing about him seems worth preserving.
He's a marker that slips from a library book

and who'll ever know who had to meet *Jenny*
at 3! or where or why the exclamation

or what pages their meeting was parting?
He's all footnotes, a boneyard of keys

at the back of the drawer as if their true
suitcases might come back to claim them.

He's all those rainy lunchtimes interleaved
between Classics and History when he'd been fourteen

for ever, working through to the last
appendix of *The Roman Empire in the East*,

to the last ragged flutter of purple
nailed to a last-ditch trading post in Asia Minor.

Some days nothing about him seems to justify
these leaps of faith: that Jenny met the one

with the key to her life; that you, dear Reader, you
might read this; that there's a hectare of stones

and goat-scrub where an old man wears a name
like *Kasar* or *Cezur* by direct succession

and his hayloft's a leafmould of edicts
rummaged from Byzantium; that the swot in the specs

might have made it past 1453. Some days
he just clings to a word, any word, say, *Trebizond*.

Tail

That's them: a soured-cream Escort
in the Tesco carpark. That's them
loading the bottle bank straight from the boot:

him and her, faces blanker
than stocking-masked bandits
as they play its holes like fruit machines,

without speaking or turning.
That's how many plonk bottles,
how many asking-a-few-friends-rounds

go down the hatch
with a blink of the flap. Smack of glass.
An after-quiver like a slammed piano.

Now the Escort nudges
into rank with fifty others,
noses in, rumps out like cows put to stud.

And now I'm waiting as the twitchy
reflex of the automatic doors
clocks them in. Let's quiz the loading bay

for clues: that leaning pagoda
of cardboard crates, the roulette sound
of a stout bottle rolling to and fro.

All circumstantial. But I'm close,
got what's left of the day
backed up against the wall

and each muffled shatter
from the bottle bank is me
ramming its head back: OK buddy,

spill the beans, thud,
are they *happy*? thud, thud, tell me
everything you know.

Thou'

Thou': a thousandth of an inch (engineering term)

A case of key and keyhole,
   us: what clicks

or doesn't in a place not seen
   until we're bits

dismantled, springs spilled everywhere;
   when edges crisp

as cornflakes once don't always kiss;
   what jams or slips

fumbled after the party, wrong door,
   sorry; what fits

in the gullet or sticks like a glove,
   depending how

precisely the spaces between us
are tooled –
          to a tolerance, let's say,
  of the nearest *thou'*.

Nineteenseventysomething

We Scotchtaped Cuban posters
round the attic walls. The wretched of the earth
made fists above us as we slept.
On damp nights they peeled slowly off
with a throat-clearing sound

like a more tactful hint than we deserved.
It was a house of all angles but right.
All the junk shops in Brighton
couldn't find furniture odd enough to fit.
Our chairs looked ill at ease, as if about to go.

When we pinned up our Indian bedspread,
pre-faded like jeans, it could have been
the clothes-horse tent I played house in
before they invented the Sixties.
Us, we'd never marry. We were outlaws

lying low, unscrewing the legs of our bed
against mother's advice. Turning back
from the smell of your body and mine
newly moistened like parched earth
I snuffed carpet dust and damp.

Nights made up most of that year .
And that voice through the wall from next door
where the curtains stayed shut.
Unseen, endless and scourging:
'Little bugger. I'll learn you...'

She was our age or less,
her four-year-old inaudible,
nearly invisible even when we saw him
and we had no words for this either
so came round to not mentioning it

but got into heavier music, Led Zep,
Wishbone Ash, and got on with the loss
of our childhoods, at leisure, urgently
before our grants ran out.
It never crossed our minds that we'd begun.

Spirit Level

Here on the sinking edge of England
the stones range from hipjoints to knucklebones.
There's a scarp drop, then the North Sea
    cants uphill and how
the tankers tightropewalk that skyline
is beyond me; I'm wobbly as the bubble
in a spirit level, ungrounded, and nothing's
    quite straight or quite true.

The Ness is a name and a notion, shifty
as the North Magnetic Pole. I've walked since teatime,
dogged as a number-crunching mainframe
        on its quest for God
rounded down to the Highest Prime Number;
the coast slips away round the corner for ever
in front and behind. It could shrug us all off
        into space: me,
this toy village with its late-night postcard shop,
this house like the fo'c'sle of a beached brigantine
with uncaulked planks that would rot in a year
        (or so the landlord says)
if it weren't for the draughts; that single car
on the front where a glow like cave moss up
from the dashboard lights two faces, lovers
        who have come to sit
and not speak and stare opposite ways.
Both ways, the sea is coming. We're crockery
slipped to the edge of a tilting table but so slowly
        who'd notice, until…?
That clatter's not the bells of Dunwich
three miles out, not the family silver being rifled,
more like cutlery shrugged into stainless-steel vats
        behind canteen roller-blinds
in a hospital no one can see their way out of,
or the school you're always back at in your dreams,
or the idea of the Self, or the United Kingdom plc,
        you know, any crumbling institution.

Nature Studies

1 *Fern Charm*

Protect us from the rage of ferns,
from the baby's clenched fist,
from the cobra's hood. From the spring

of the set trap, from the slippy
grip-curl of octopus limbs,
protect us. Say *Hart's-tongue*

Hart's-tongue as if words
might lick the newborn
season into shape. Protect us

from the spring.

2 *Foxgloves at Dungeness*

Zero
minus one... Ignition
and a blaze of purple
powering up...

Green bud-tips,
all that thrust
beneath them, hang
on the critical seconds

of lift-off,
on a whim of windspeed,
between hungry earth
and empty sky.

3 *Dragonfly Tanka*

Oil-film wings, false depths
in its hologram eyes, dead
still: a gold-wire brooch
for you... At a touch, it rips
off, like a lit fuse, sizzling.

4 *Sundew*

Drops of honeyspit
between the sundew's teeth.

A forty poster bed
pink-lit velvety green,

fringed, musky. fly,
he fancies he can see

himself, shrink-wrapped
in surface tension,

in each globe of mucus,
whole and looking out;

he fancies it could be
a gem, a gift for her.

Or her, or her. Eternity,
he'll say, a solitaire.

5 *Limpets at Wylfa*

One tense: the present.
One will : to grip.
One muscle clenched.
   One shell
that grinds to fit
the facts of stone.
One story time
    will tell.

Beach Party

Just a little too much, maybe, of everything
a beach should have: miles,
bleached as a salt pan and flat as forever.

In long-shot, a dune buggy seems to come
and come straight on and gets no nearer,
riding the bucks and the slumps,

sand spattering hindwards, doggie-fashion.
Whines of wheelspin join the littler squeals
of party animals. The wide-screen backdrop

has lavender mud tints like the veins of eyelids.
(You could market it as *Twilight*.)
Now, a touch of blusher. Nightfall

ups the treble, cuts the bass.
Their laughter goes like oystercatchers
winking out of range; their headlight beam

is trying to prise the dark up like a stone.
It stalls and goes dim. All round,
a faint prickling sigh

like metal cooling: wormcasts,
pocks and pores. The water table darkens upwards,
raising salts like a mineral dream

and razor shells and crab backs
blemishing the clean sweep
like those longship burials in sand

that nothing but their slight impurities
give definition and, as soon as seen,
dry, bleach and blow away.

A Detail from Bosch

Meadow cranesbill, tiny monster,
a stork's head in plant form...
and I'm back in the Garden

of Earthly Delights, in Sundays
at Aunt Bea's, never-ended – *say*
Thank You, say Please –

and the cave-dripping tut of her clock.
I hid behind her sofa
with The World's Great Paintings,

guiltily possessed by
(worse than Playboy) those live
strutting bagpipe bladders,

the dismantled hangar of that torso,
head still smiling as it turned.
The cruelty: how all flesh, stripped down,

might become something other,
and Aunt Bea's plucked neck
one of the ones I saw

hung by their claws in Mack the butcher's;
how a life could come
to pecking old grit, the stab of a kiss

I winced from, cruelly.

Dry
(St Michan's crypt, Dublin)

Smiles not to be argued with,
queasing me forward... *Go on,*
he won't bite. Each tour on the hour
had to proffer a child
to the side of his thin box bed.
The grown-ups rippled,
clockwork gathering to strike.

I stood; he lay
as befitted our stations, him
six hundred years my senior,
Sir No-one-now, Knight. The hand
he granted to me like a favour
(glossed with other people's sweat)
felt like a Guy's twig glove.

I'd glued Airfix models
with more life to them than this:
canvas skin, bone struts,
just a stiff-necked refusal
quite to be a skeleton.
The flashbulbs winced.
The guide held out her palm.

I thought of this today
in the woods after rain, in a clearing
of sawdust and sunlight.
There was the mystery: steam
from a cut stump mingling up
into all shapes and none, life,
a pan boiling dry.

A Scorcher

Walk, don't jog: it's official.
Don't let the kids play out.
Don't breathe the air. Reactions
simmered in a pan of ozone smog

dissolve our boundaries; across the *life/
not-life* line molecules begin to fraternise
like a breaking of ranks in the trenches.
So we cough and slow.

We cover up. Overexposed
we check for shadows on the skin.
In the ultraviolet light of what we know
the future begins to look pale

as the Middle Ages. Grey-faced girls
with thighs no wider than their knees
appear in our midst now
like omens of famine, bruise-eyed

like the worn-down wives
they'd rather die than be.
And we learn to adapt. Betray
no more than awkward sympathy

when someone's toddler in the crowded bus
fights a strangle of asthma,
scrabbling and slipping on each breath
like a loosening scree.

Persons Unknown

This is the Pier Point Hotel and they

are the only residents.
It's more exclusive now than 5-star

since the Council whacked up hardboard
on the downstairs, and the UNSAFE STRUCTURE sign.

The Receiver's got his hands full, what
with weighing an antheap of debts

against goods that get less with each slither
of shale, each crump of a wave on the cliff.

It was a wet night they teased back the wire
just enough for a calor gas stove and a bedroll

and themselves. By morning the flit of them
at an upstairs window and that cat-at-the-back-door

baby's cry was proof, if proof were needed:
once land starts slipping it goes to the bad,

good riddance. Remember how the Clifftop Bar
broke out in an acne of under-age drinking

and the landlord took to serving in his vest,
his cheeks rusting from the inside like a wreck

at high-water? Now these fly-by-night squatters
had a cranked-out bus, one with sacks on the windows

and a dog like frayed wire, didn't they? Well, no,
but these things soon appeared

somewhere nearby where no one could see them.

*

It may be the Pier Point Hotel but you

don't figure, you're a blank
on the inventory. You
among fixtures and fittings

like the cherry plush bar
with its paunched look, its buttons
gone missing like teddy bears' eyes.

Yes, you, putting your boots up
in the cork tiled alcoves,
you, squelching the pump handles

(marked with a price per pint
that nails their last pull to the month
sure as carbon dating.)

Kicking the steel kegs, you,
you'd sup the dregs, you'd spoon them
to the baby when it creaks by night.

Why don't you answer? Or appear
at a balcony window like royalty, to bless us
with a V-sign? Thanks to you

folk lie awake all hours, listening
for the raves you must surely
foment out of nowhere

like maggots in meat. Why can't we hear?

*

Final guests of the Pier Point Hotel we

go on tiptoe for no reason.
Or spread arms and whoosh
down the corridor laughing
as if there were maids stepping out

from every bedroom, tea things
shocked up off their trays
like a clatter of doves.
But the kid can't be left

in a room stacked with bust chairs
and pieces of bidet, where moonlight
still winkles out glass from the floorboards
or flatters the gold-look

of a wire record rack
full of *Swing with the Sixties
Volume 3*. We can't talk
but must whisper or shout,

and the closer we bundle to sleep,
the more apart we seem.
Last night each of us thought we woke
to find the other missing

and knew where to look: through the door
we shouldn't open to the Clifftop Bar,
with no window, no frame and no wall
where the mould-patterned Axminster frays

in a bite like stringy celery.
At our feet, a faint whicker of gulls...
A few slipped off to circle leisurely
as cream in stirred coffee. Beneath

rose a pale blotch of foam.
When I was small in bed
I'd squeeze my eyelids tight,
half afraid of the space in my head

where the nebulas came like that and kept on coming.

Postcards, West Bay

(after a photograph by Martin Parr)

These are the last days. And these are the signs.
       And nothing is by chance.
These are the cards, the Tarot of the times.
       We shuffle, heads bent,
round the white wire racks. These wayside shrines.

These icons. Faithfulness on its settee
       is figured by The Poodle
gazing where the coal-look fire must be,
       his master's voice. The same
fire lights The Fluffy Kitten's eyes, though she

is a type of the Snow Leopard, captured
       at the entrails of her prey,
a party streamer tangle. Here is The Thatcher
       on the crest of his new fire risk,
hand raised like the poodle's paw. What rapture

is prepared for him, for all who understand
       the correspondences: the buffed-
up green steam locomotive and the two-in-hand
       plough team converging
on a final point? The point is where we stand

in late light, colours heightened, sights for sore
       eyes, eczema'd.
Salve us. Everything we see is slightly raw.
       Don't scratch the surface,
it'll scar. Who made the red shift, and what for,

what hopes and brochures drew us to West Bay
       (Look to the West. The West
declines.) and booked us in and made us stay
       and made us see how everything
bleeds, bleed, these last days, bleeds away.

A Liminal State

(Estonia, September 1994)

1 *Documentary*

Five Aeroflot sky-tubs by the lumpy runway
sport blue-and-white paint now: ESTONIAN AIR.
Like gulls with a storm in the offing
they face the same way at the wind.

There are trains cut in half at the border
like worms; an independent engine
pulls out from the platform while its rolling stock
stays Russian. Lines have to be drawn

like today: PAKA *(bye for now,*
not quite *adieu)* flyposts most walls
with a Red Army helipad cap, a walrus neck
that seems an easy target from behind.

Like kids with their parents' cameras
there are families posed edgily outside
the place people tried not to mention,
with a name plate saying anything but KGB.

The barracks is a film set waiting
for a new producer and a cast of thousands.
The windows are kicked out from the inside,
bunk rooms trashed. Here's half a skip of uniforms.

Round the base, there's been a fly-buzz of types
in leather jackets all this last year,
men in a small way of business but expanding
and with foreign friends. Out there in the bay

ochre hulks have faced home up the Gulf of Finland
for months as if waiting the word.
(The Moscow-Tallinn post goes quicker
these days via London.)

Beneath the stained ziggurat
of the Olympic Pride yachting complex
a sharp Finnish hydrofoil suns its wings.
A car ferry trots out in the team's new colours

and is not yet anybody's news.

A nod, in passing, to the scar
in the park where all the paths
        converge on nothing
but a ten-foot concrete square
gouged up like a bad extraction,
shreds of tooth, steel nerve-ends
        sheared off proud
to the ground, not safe for children.
It nags like the place where the pain
has been and gone, the lost limb
        still tapping its fingers,
still humming the old refrain.

There's a clutch of Lenins in the cellar
of the town museum, faced everywhichway
        to the future, some reclining,
most declaiming, deafly. Quite a conspiracy...
Still, their splintered soles would slot
back onto the scars of their plinths
        snug as a numb foot
in a snowboot. They're kept, no, not
just in case, for as long as it takes
for History to lose that old capital H
        like a crime on its head,
for all this to be lower-case, just history.

One night the Bronze Age began. A van
skulked up an alley finger-picking clean
        every public memorial.
Slogans stuttered into silence. Scrap men
made a killing. The great names and dates
lost their memory, letter by letter,
        leaving pinholes in the slabs
like Braille, or the undeciphered script
in the newly-excavated sanctum, which might
if you let your focus blur, just fall
        into pattern and sense.
Might be a curse, the writing on the wall.

3 *Liminal*

The rackety bus has shaken us down
like a washing machine soothes fretful

babies, down to there-there mutterings
on the edge of sleep, so low I can't tell

which is Estonian, which Russian. Straight
cut through flat land, the road's as dull

as the proof that Zeno's arrow never strikes.
There's a tree without a trunk, a stonepile

like a reef, in low mist. Puddles
of brightness rise as darkness falls,

in measure like a physical equation.
Memories of marsh seep back, subliminal,

till it's white to the black rim of woods
under darkening blue, like the national

flag. In one already-changing moment
droplet after droplet casts its individual

vote to be mist. The road is a causeway
waiting for a wave of it to curl

up and over. Now. We hit the brightness
and we're in it and it's gloom and chill

and half the night to go. The driver hums
to keep awake, no words, all

low throat voice, no tune.

4 *Heart Stones*

The driver pulls us over
somewhere north of Poltsamaa
to introduce us to a stone
    as if it was royalty.

He shuts off the engine
and turns, gravely beaming.
Ten thousand boulders
in a tiny land but one, this one,
no other, is transfigured
    by grace of (surer than verse)
    geometry: dead-centre,
    the heart of the homeland
though there's not a house in sight.
If those disputed hectares in the east
were ceded, would this centre hold?
    Would they trundle it west in a truck?
    At once the fields around look papery,
    crumpled, a map stroked out flat
with this boulder for paperweight,
and a stiff wind riffling at the edges.
A slap and a rip and it could fly away.

          *

    Turn aside from the dull road to Narva,
    down the bank: those puddles of stones,
waist deep, grey overlapping rings
like lichen, with nothing to tell them
    from every field's scraped-up pile
    like dustpan sweepings – nothing
but what's walled precisely at the core.
There, a two-metre fridge-freezer box
    for the big cheese with his gravegoods.
    Here, suitcase size,
twin matching gaps in the bloodline,
nobody's ancestors. It's the spaces
    at the heart that place us, not the edge
    that crumbles as the freight rolls by.

5 *International Relations*

The deep-pile hush
of moss. All round us
tingling resonance of spruce.
I can't utter a word
for fear it lasts and lasts.

'You English,' she says,
'I can't tell from American
these days, always rushing in
to *share* your feelings.
This *heart on the sleeve*

(is that right?) can't still
be beating... *Friendship?*
The official word for occupation.
Give me fifty years
to lose the taste of it,

I'm sorry...' And later:
'No wonder your Americans
and Russians understand each other
like the best of enemies.
They're so alike,

the type who invite you,
surprise! to a party
in your own house.
If you say you have a headache
they look hurt – *sincerely* –

         then kick down the door...'

6 *Scorched Earth*

A year or two
of thistles uncut
and it's theirs:

first, nettles
at the borders, bramble
tripwires, then birches

like fingers of dazzle
prising in between
the warping timbers

to a hayloft's
warm biscuity dark.
Too white, those trees

stepping in over marginal land
between the forest
and the straight-ruled wheat –

too bright, as if
they sucked light up
to flare it off

like a Statue-of-Liberty
torch at the oil works,
smoke by day and fire by night,

and the earth at their feet
too dark-grained
fifty years on – the ash

of hayloft, house and barn
feeding grass, feeding
birch and bramble, feeding

thistles as sharp as a cough
in a theatre's hush
before the next act starts.

7 *Forest Brother*

(*Metsavennad:* Forest Brothers – resistance fighters
against the Soviet occupation of 1944)

Consider the last of the Forest Brothers

thirty years behind bars
of spruce or white birch trunks
that look like a cage from any angle.
Thirty years of melting through.

Of nesting in the needly itch
like the last of a species
listed as extinct
but still with a price on his pelt.

Of the plush smell of mushrooms
on the edge of rotting
and the rush-matting drift
underfoot and the moss,

such a hush, just a cough
and the wood catches cold.
Consider living like a mouse
in the soundbox of a violin

among the wind's harmonics,
being what isn't there
at the edge of the clearing
when the dogs bark and the farmer

chooses not to hear. His war
comes down to this: to be a dream,
a bad one, moving in the corner
of the vision of a dawn

that has abolished shadows.
Do dreams itch? Catch cold?
Or look up by a river,
with a rucksack and a leather jacket

grinning at two fishermen
who pass the time of day
and then produce a camera, smile!
and then their KGB credentials.

August Sabe. 1979.
His last word is a gulp of air
in the pool where he jumped
and stayed under. Consider him

then consider the last
Forest Brother but one, who died
some time earlier, thinking
'There's still Sabe' – him

with no name, no photograph,
so much more rare
because he could be anyone...

Back in the bad old days
    I had a job – to say everything
        no one else would. And they listened
like kids in a Whispering Gallery
    half afraid of their own voices
        scuttling round blank walls and back.
I said too much, of course.
    Even a little was too much –
        these were the bad old days, remember –
and when the silencers came
    my hush rippled through crowds;
        when I passed down the street
folk turned to listen.
    Ah, the bad old days. Now
        I can leave a silence and...

That was one, did you notice it?
    No?
        Then I'll say it again.

9 *Postsoviet Postmodern*
Vaike-Oismae, Tallinn

Launched by the Soviet Sixties, this scheme
for a suburb in concentric rings says moon-base,
says orbiting station: a hand-me-down dream
    from American sci-fi. Remember the Space Race?
    Cosmonauts on launchpads in the Khazakh
    dust, pot-roasted secretly at the state's
discretion? Now we wake to stains and cracks,
the creep of concrete cancer much the same
as relicts of the Sixties anywhere: Caracas,
    Wandsworth. But vineberry swarms up to claim
    ten storey cliffs, each creeper a ripped seam
    of autumn. Each block wears a shirt of flame.

The Pumping Station's down again; half
Tallinn's hot taps gurgle dry. I'm in an eighth
floor flat, bussed to a cousin's for a bath.
    On TV, a Mexican dream of L.A.: ghost-
    Spanish moves the lips. Curt as an epitaph,

Estonian subtitles. Russian, dubbed almost
in synch. Slipped through cracks in the scene
a stray *porque?* like a weed in a pavement. My host
has left *Women's Day: Australia's Biggest Magazine*
        (from other cousins) where I'll see. *'Aussie Man Relates*
        Penis Mutilation' 'Diana – Sexpot Or Ice Queen?'
        with a Japanese remote control for paperweight.

Outside, there's scrub encroaching. Waste ground.
A cow at a stake. A dirt track. And a frontier
with what's gone. That low grassed-over mound
        should be a long barrow, but the door
        is dented steel – a reinforced surround,
        a man-sized catflap. Now we're echoes in a corridor,
an air-raid-shelter hush one step could detonate,
but lined with lock-ups, dozens, like a bullion store.
Ours rattles up, bumping its counterweight,
        a cylinder block, and there's the family car,
        the great grey Lada like a warrior in state
        among shelves racked with gravegoods, jar on jar
of gherkin flesh crammed into murky green.
Lab specimens. And garnet glints: a ruined bar
of bottles – vodka, 'Churchill's London Gin' –
        transfused with redcurrant juice, like every year
        in every farm's earth-cellar till the history machine
        crashed from the sky and left us stranded here.

Babble

He never asked –
how could he? –
but it came with him,
the gift of tongues,

and they clustered around
as if astounded,
total strangers bending
to his buggy in the street.

Those with ears to hear
might spot Inuit gutturals,
sheaves of Slavonic *tsh* or *tsch*,
a glottal click of Xhosa

tangled like all our routes
out of Africa, forkings of tongues
into deltas and floodplains.
They became afraid

and held up things,
simple and solid to cling to.
Teddy, they said, *baby,*
mouthing slow and clear

like trained negotiators
hotlined to the penthouse
where he'd holed up, Howard Hughes
of the Babel Hotel

amongst hung gardens
and the hammering of gastarbeiter
workmen; some nights
a whole storey gives way;

in the morning there's scaffolding,
power tools, Michael Jackson songs
in Turkish, all channels at once
on their trannies. No wonder

that there comes a day
he chucks it in, throwing the switch
to cut whole sectors into darkness,
silence, and comes down

to their smiles and their camcorders
whirring like the press corps
when his lips or tongue chance
on a *Ma* or *Da*.

Kleep

Think of the birds flying south for the winter, cranes for
instance. They fly on and on and on, and it doesn't matter
what ideas, big or small, they may have buzzing around inside
their heads, they'll still keep on flying...They fly on and on,
and what if they do throw up a philosopher? Let them keep
their philosophy, so long as they don't stop flying.

Toozenbach in Chekhov's THREE SISTERS

...or if one of them snagged
   on the frizzly invisible wire
      of a satellite wavelength
that happened to fill
   the hollows of his beak and skull
      with questions
as the flock closed up and flickered on,
   this one piece
      flaking off and dropping
on a rain-slicked car park –
   an avocet, one,
      like a whole new thought
expelled from the mind that hatched it:

what if all this, this snoot of a bill,
   this flashback of black and white
      flagged up as we rise off water,
each scoop-and-stilt twist
   of the genes, were nothing
      but containers for the word
kleep   kleep
   as it tells us like beads
      on its flightpaths, day and night
speeding up to the flutter
   of movietone monochrome,
      no intermission, just a soundtrack
playing on and on to empty stalls?

The Language of the Bird People

unmoved
out on the edge of utter
North
     of utter
         utter...
             (try again)

unmoved
thin as lace-

makers' bobbins
their limb-silhouettes

against a grey lake
in their punts of bark so flat

they might be standing on the water
they compose an alphabet

with the tilt of a spear
the coil of a cast net

splash
though all that reaches here

at the edge is ripples
broad and shallow

truckling at a boulder
a stipple of reeds

like a visible rumour
then again

the peewit cries they scratch
on the frosted glass of morning

once an hour maybe
unmoving is a message

cut in lapidary style
that spells precisely nothing

we can hope   but try
again   to guess

'Cult objects: Neolithic proto-
Finno-Ugric'
                a bird-headed ladle
                the rim of a bowl
incised with Diver Pintail Grebe
each reduced
                to an ideogram
                a glyph   a rune
ten species of Z evolving to
                pure attitude

'A religion of waterfowl, presumably'
the reappearing
                W or V of geese
                like a sign in the sky
ragged edge of the season's much-
patched garment
                that they stitch
                back into place
with needling cries   to make do
                for another year

Don't credit the tale
that they followed the wild-
fowl north so far
they left speech behind

like a Victorian explorer's
folding table, candlesticks and cloth
abandoned almost sadly
by the last defecting porter.

But whistles and caws
are sharper warnings, honks and chirrups
more companionable
for meaning only that.

Don't think their poets
whittled nightingale cadenzas.
No, picture them rapt
in a darkening ring

by the sound of one goose
cronking with a micro-tonal
change of pitch
less than a warping of windspeed

till in a trance beyond boredom
they were seized
by the wonder of distance, thoughts
teased into cirrus-thin threads.

On a poor night they might plan
new destinations; on a good one,
woken by a rush of wings,
might find the poet gone.

strakings of cirrus

the windpaths
down which birds will come

today?   no

till the folk brim full of it
this lacking something

and the wide high sky

is one turbulent stream
of not arriving

the cloud teased to slaloming tracks

prickling smitters of sand
swerving over a beach

a live white shadow

they squint north
as if they could see

in the switch and tease

of wind direction
something   something

call it home

'Tenth night out: serious tundra, bog-
quaking soft. Lashed guyropes to stones.
No chat. By this stage of an expedition
talking's as much of a slog
       as walking, and less use. Dusk was a seep
       of grey light downwards, puddling in a tarn
       edged with boulders, crosshatched with reeds.
       The other men clocked into sleep

and missed it: up over the moor
from the south, a creaking
like a waggon being trundled, then
as sudden as the kicking open of a door
       the tarn was a clamour, a claque
       in the front stalls of darkness,
       each separate syllable insisting
       on itself, a shopfloor clang and crack

of hammering out the likeness
of a language. A raw spring of speech.
I stumbled out, my torch beam stubbing
into bristling wings like the pikes
    of a pitchfork rebellion as their outcry spread
    across the water, circles shuddering
    out and all the voices leaving and the Word,
    if word it was, unsaid...'

At some point on the road north,
a divorce
and another and another...
Steps to more crisp articulation.

One group holds north-west
is the true way of the birdpaths,
one hears the wind in the east.
A turn of speech

might sway a council
like a change in the breeze,
one leading to a sibilance of spruces,
one to the vowel of a duck cry,

while the dumb Ob
widens its swerves into marshland
without end or definition.
The Nenets. The Komi. The Khanty.

Each arrives at a name, one word
finally uttered. At the logging camp
an old man washing pans
feeds a girl from the Institute's

microphone with syllables
from his grandmother's larder.
He steals the cassete player
for his nephews in Murmansk

and the end of the line
is a footnote. The Udmuts.
The Mordvin. The Mansi.
Did they know they'd arrived

and there was nothing for it but to wait,
unmoving, for the chainsaws
ruling a new edge to the forest,
new smoke rising, uttered

once, and losing definition
as it thins towards them
like geese of a dwindling species
trying for true North

                              again
                                    again?

That Grave, Heptonstall Churchyard
(for TB)

I'm not here now; you've never been
        and she?
She's here in name. Put in her place.
All round her, life on life's defined
        by family:

Beloved Husband... Wife Of The Above...
        And dates,
the years from *Sadly Missed* to *Reunited.*
Here it's life that puts asunder; death
        consolidates

but still needs edging. There's a splashy blurt
        of strimmer. Smells
of cut green. Her plot's earth, no kerb,
a give-and-take of weeds along the border.
        Now the bells

blur, two notes slipping out of phase
        that jar
like two tongues round one language, half
a tone apart, like English and American
        in you, in her –

half rhymes, the way your lips make *marry*
        sound like *merry.*
So the continental drift of vowels
and lives breeds ironies, which epitaphs
        are meant to bury.

I'm not here, not now, but writing this
        upstairs, alone
and with you, also not here, in the way
that words can do, the kind that won't be
        set in stone.

Around the church graves lie like hatches
        battened down.
In place. Does she belong? Do we? Where
else could these thoughts be at home but on
        disputed ground?

Mock Orange

Keep it, he thought, and watch it wither.
A controlled experiment.

A tissue sample, tested
to destruction. Science against sentiment.

It was limp in a week; in a month,
crisp as a wing case in the spider's nook;

in two, a Haversham gown
already, with that age-scorched look,

no scent, so little body
to its parchment, the touch of a pen

would destroy it. There, it's gone.
But it's not. He starts over again.

                *

Evaluate. Record. Two, three hours of seminar.
A working lunch. A breath outside,
and a throwaway line, a dare, and there they are

with a sprig each from someone else's garden;
back for two, three hours more
of what he can't remember, can't remember anything

except how she twirled hers, absently,
stroking the curve of her throat while listening,
down to the dip between the collar bones. He

found his still in his hand, and hid it, coming home.

*

Keep it, he thought, and watch it wither.
Now it's scentless, colourless,
QED, stick to science; resist
temptation to play alchemist,

to pound it in a mortar, to a white
dust potent as cocaine,
the flower of albescence, something
dying for a change.

No, let it wither, husks of flight
like the butterfly wings
good children used to save to press
into pictures of quite other things,

ball gowns, waterfalls – that
was the art of it. Under glass
they're antiques now, and the children
more gone than the butterflies. Let it pass...

*

...or with its own dried twig
like a pin through the thorax,
classify it. But tonight it's him
the collector who's nailed to the page,
squirming, just out of reach

of his numbing formaldehyde,
while the wings of all the moments
caught, or not quite, whisper
in the air around him, taunting.
One brushes his cheek.

Sweet Bird

Rare, yes, but what could she do with it?
On some other island those flashes of aqua,
viridian, bleeding-heart cerise
might be bridal tokens or hard currency.
Nothing convertible here.

It hunched on her windowsill. Hungry?
Hurt? She put out a saucer and scraps.
What if it was a protected species;
if it died, who'd be liable?
She'd ease it back to the wild...

It flew up to a treetop. Twitched about
once like a compass needle. Dropped
from sight. Back home,
it had got there before her,
draped across the table like a poacher's pheasant

asking to be trussed and hung. Or mounted,
though she'd never been the trophy type.
By the phone off the hook she could see
it had been at the Yellow Pages;
the taxidermist was already on his way,

a home call, with scalpel and bodkin
and sealable bags. He wouldn't be fobbed off.
Someone would be a collector's piece
before the night was out. But love, *love*
love, it sang, as if that was all there was to say.

Love and Co.

Down the rabbit hole, now, in no time, as
your eyes lock, before you can think
It could happen, it has:

the old voice-over. You,
it whispers, swish as automatic doors,
could be that holiday for two,

both your lives left well
behind, still going round without you
like suitcases on the airport carousel.

Take this one-in-a-lifetime chance
of a timeshare. (It's a fenced-off plot
where the dust-devils dance

through the wire.) Catch the wink
of a gold tooth when the sales rep smiles,
that handshake fastened with a clink

of rings borrowed from several hands.
Done. Before you can think.

Hungry Ghosts in Happy Eater

One stage on the Tibetan Wheel of Life is occupied by the Hungry Ghosts;
with huge stomachs and tiny mouths, they can never satisfy their hungers.

These two, wanting so much
they could eat each other
up, all up
and they'd be gone

leaving what
for the damage assessors,
the investigators,
but a napkin

crumpled like the story of a life
neatly dropped on a plate
and food uneaten
and the bill unpaid

and two chairs facing,
empty to the brim
with wants
like the guests

at a spoilt kid's party
wide-eyed
as the rabbit-mould
pink jelly, cut,

slumps like a last
chance missed
to tense and twitch
and leap away?

Time Lapse

Already going, it may have been gone
    before he'd raised a glass –
        absent friends:

the midnight that wouldn't be hers
    for eight hours yet was off
        sweeping west,

sweeping brilliant moments, congas, party
    popper tangle, fireworks falling,
        Auld Lang Syne

into its bin bag; off-road, over hills now, over
    cloggy levels and the shot-silk silt fields
        of the estuary,

a radio mast, a lightship rocked by the Atlantic.
    Sweeping foam tips up like sawdust,
        broken glass

and resolutions, now it panned its beam
    of dark across, a time-zone wide,
        not remembering

him to her or anyone to anyone, as if
    forgetting was its job. A year
        between us now,

he thought, and what if time, once slipped,
    went on slipping? If he slept
        he might open his eyes

to find it decades or a different life,
    a bed round which, uneasy,
        unfamiliar

wife and children watch him wake, afraid
    as for a moment he can't
        recollect himself.

Tact
(Dr Sun-Yat-Sen Garden, Vancouver)

A floating leaf pokes up its head,
a lacquered eye stripe, and becomes a terrapin.
    Each pebble is deliberate:
sharp/white for yang, smooth/black for yin.

Outside the tile-topped walls a crane,
wires, intersection lights... Inside, waist high
    raddled limestone
in a tank of stillness – bonsai

mountains. Though if those
are mountains how huge are the carp that rise
    through the pools? And me?
A giant suddenly embarrassed by his size.

Can't budge... till in the courtyard,
slow as dancing underwater, Tai Chi Chuan
    unwraps the movements of its doers
like an endless present. One young man,

sea-urchin-haired, with droopy dungarees
unhitched on one side, stoops and sweeps and smooths
        the space around him. Out,
    along his gaze, the movement moves

    beyond his finger-tips, a cast
coil, as if silt-thick eddies veered and stirred
        the liquid time has slowed to.
    Tact: to be, precisely, when a word

    might break the surface tension
like a not-yet-lover's not-quite-accidental touch,
        the shudder that runs through a life
    and moves on, out. I've said too much.

Underside

Lit from below

the pale grey-green of lichen,
our faces drift away

and away from ourselves
much as our rowboat drifts

beneath this shallow arch
that has stalactite dewlaps already.

In a hush like a studio
suddenly on air, a drip

sends its ripples out
up from under our faces

and this low vault and the blades
of our shipped and still dribbling oars,

the way we play stray lights
across each other – threat or love

like the flash of a car in the street
riffled back through a chink in the curtains...

Yes, but quite indifferently.
I can't help looking for the spot

where long after the drop
the rings keep coming

into being, light
out of dark out of light,

although you'd think there's nothing there.

Gargangel

It began as a creaking, an ache in my stone
thews. There's a word for you,
since words are all I've got from over-
looking centuries: gossip, hey-nonny-no
and paternoster. Acid rain and organ wheeze
had worn me down to bone and horn and wing,

to a crick in the neck and a joke of a wing
like a broken umbrella. Still, to be set in stone
seemed like a future. Whose clever wheeze
was it to set me trembling? And did you
so much as frisk your hair or look up, downcast? No,
it could have been a small cloud passing over,

my shadow touching you. Then it was over
until, after dark, the first twinge in my wing,
a thin sinew unlocking. No, I said, no,
I've seen it: crash; next morning, shattered stone
and the precinct taped off. Not me, thank you.
Figures my age are meant to spout and wheeze

but not like this, not this bump-start wheeze
inside my ribs. I thought all that was over
centuries ago, that ridiculous *It could be you…*
from empty skies: *How long since an angel wing-
beat last rattled the stained glass? Stone
the crows, what are you made of?* Could I say *No,*

leave me to crouch and crumble slowly? No!
I struggled upright, with a rip and wheeze,
uprooted, with a shower of dust and stone
and for a moment I swayed, teetering over
the stomach-punch drop, then unfurled a wing
and launched out, where else but towards you,

amazed, aloft, alone, as much I as you are you.
Dipping badly over Pulteney Street, no
turning back now, I cranked up a wing
beat, stiff, slow, with a whistle like the wheeze
of pigeon panic. No one looked up as I passed over
homing on your sill, your narrow window, stone

clunking stone and clinging, peering in – and saw you
squinting up, over your reading glasses. Now! But no,
I squ-squ-wheeze but can't fit in, can't fold this wing.

Hanging Garden

If I did it again, it would have to be there

in Devonian Gardens, in the warp and weft
        of downtown Calgary.

The street map's not much use. That square
        of green; it's nowhere, literally,

on earth. Get there, the sign points skywards.
        You'd come, wouldn't you,

in white, beside me, in the stainless lift,
        slipping up its glass tube

snug as the plunger in a hypodermic?
        Three, four storeys high

among mirrorshade windows pixelating
        one another and the sky,

a seasick sway as gravity relaxes, then
    we'd step out, you and I,

into rainforest. Insect fibrillations. Fountains
    like whippy ice cream.

In the recycled plosh, dazed koi. The garden,
    hanging, cradled by technology,

held for its own protection in a girder cage
    with all workings exposed,

no pretence: thrumming ducts thick as dustbins,
    fan-blowers in rows

sigh like jet engines trundling to takeoff,
    fan blades idling, as if this

were aircraft, hangar *and* departure lounge.
    Any moment now, the shift

of pitch, the surge, the caught breath. Squeeze
    my hand, whoever you might be,

and lead me past the crimson rope, the Private
    Function sign, where hourly

the brides and the grooms take their places
    and glow, and something

like the first time ever is preserved; photographers
    make summer lightning

and glimpsed through undergrowth are faces, some
    just passing, some returning

day after day among the spikes and fronds
    and bougainvillea to yearn in,

it could be at us. My unknowable future,
    what couldn't we swear

in all innocence? Yes, we'd say, yes.
    It would have to be there.

Fosse Way, Grey Day

Slap rapeseed yellow
on a drystone landscape,
a coat of new gloss that will peel

when the subsidies shift.
Paint it up to the edge
of the skyline, the Camp

that's a worn-down reef of green,
a sandbar where no end of history
has grounded. A flat wheeze:

that's Norbert Dentressangle hauling up
to the Chariot's Rest for diesel,
off the straight way there and back

where every stop seems halfway:
the new ditch and rampart
round the lay-by where the gypsies were last year,

car-carcases and chrome trim,
bleeds of oil in the long grass;
or Luke's Griddle Bar trailer

with its flap up, bottles in a row
like an apothecary's, ketchup red,
brown Daddy's, mustard

spry as rapeseed or the froth
of stonecrop suddenly
as sunlight, yellow out of grey.

Ground Control

A gust, and the skyline is bristling with them,
cloud-slip behind them and wild blue bluster,
and what are they hefting, one-handed like butlers

with trays of champagne flutes? Blades
of six-foot wingspans like well-balanced spears,
light as bird bone, and damsel fly bodies, cerise,

white, kingfisher, lime. Up close, it is a tribe
of married-looking men in specs and mufflers,
like a Scout troop from the Fifties. With the bluff

drop at their feet, the motorway miles down,
and the wind, they take a roll call, surnames only
then step to the edge. At the whistle they go,

leaning forwards, balancing each model glider
on the air, nose up, nose down, to teeter,
then edge out of reach. Out of whisper.

A single line sketch of itself, one turns
as easily as frisking over in your sleep to run
downwind, shaving the ridge, and the men

come tracking downhill at a slant, in pairs,
across heather and ash and burnt gorse curls
and violets. With black box and whiskery aerial,

eyes on the sky, each one trusts the other's
two hands on his waist to steer him, leaning
heads together, whispering like secrets

where to, and where now to, put his feet.

Changes of Address

After he left
it was the change-of-address slips
that came from everywhichwhere now and then;

it was the way he made you fill
whole pages of address book with him,
him scored out again and again,

like drafts of himself he had to mail you,
brief as haiku and never quite right.
It was the postcards from what might have been

a holiday, with here and there a 'we'
unexplained, that might be the family, the wife,
the lover or the zeitgeist; most recently,

this e-mail with a page-and-a-half
of cc's like the credits at the end
of a low budget film, and where he's @

is somewhere that is no place.
So a pulse from the receding stars
prints out as constellations on our flat

earth minds, although they're years
of light apart, and separate. It was,
it is, the way he wants it known

how far he's got...but who's to mark
this correspondence course, this
distance learning, in...what: *Home*

as a Foreign Language?

Summerhouse Sauna

(Estonia, 1997)

Men, we don't touch.
Even a handshake is a brisk clunk
like a gear change –
the crisper, the less ground lost.

Here there's nothing between us.
See our buttock-marks in sweat
flank to flank on the wooden slat shelf.
We're racked like loaves in an oven;

this could be some lesser waiting-room
in Hell, lit by the glimmer
of the bow-legged stove
that squats like a grudge in armour.

A dip of the copper ladle
in the bucket, a splash on the pigs
of scrap iron that stand in for stones,
and steam takes us all by the throat.

For a moment we're boggle-eyed
all in the same no-language.
The first word anyone has breath for
is a victory and goes down like a joke.

Outside, we lope down to a pool
edged in bin-liner black
as if we'd evaded the hunt. Unmanned,
scrotum shrunk to a prune,

we gasp, duck and come up to mist
in the birches, that sparkles the skin
of the pond, and our own pink as babies.
We could start again from here.